Subaltern Linguistics

Subaltern Linguistics challenges the goals and theoretical foundations of colonial linguistics, academia, and education and provides alternative approaches and practices. The goal of subaltern practice is to create economies, projects, and resources that can be made and used by community members and leaders to develop and promote community beneficial projects in their own language (or a language of their choice). In doing subaltern and CREDIBLE work, we need to develop a new array of tools and resources. This book provides a broad introduction to how this can be done along with examples of multiple CREDIBLE projects carried out by students and members of the broader community.

The textbook is divided into four parts. In Part I, we establish the need for this work, introduce some concepts that the CREDIBLE approach draws on, and explain what we mean by CREDIBLE projects. In Part II, we share what can be done when we adopt a CREDIBLE approach, including several examples of student projects across a range of areas such as education, environment, healthcare, and economic development. Part III provides detailed guidelines and instructions on how to develop CREDIBLE projects with worksheets and activities that can be used to conceptualise, plan, and develop CREDIBLE projects. Finally, Part IV includes four CREDIBLE project reports as examples of how this work can be written up for wider dissemination.

This text is an essential guide to a new way of doing linguistics, reflecting the diversity and richness of today's world.

Ahmar Mahboob, also known as Sunny Boy Brumby and Prof Nomad, is Associate Professor in the Faculty of Social Sciences at the University of Sydney. They were recognised as field leader in English language and literature by the Australian Magazine in 2019 and their poetry was inducted into the Australian Poetry Hall of Fame, Guyra, NSW, in 2021. They are the founding Editor-in-Chief of the upcoming Routledge Resource Online: English in the Real World.

Aurelie Mallet holds a PhD in Linguistics from the University of Sydney. She has a focus on medical discourse, in particular public health discourse. Her PhD utilised the principles of Positive Discourse Analysis to deconstruct and analyse Australia's successful National Tobacco

Campaign, leading to the proposal of a new campaign targeting excessive sugar. Aurelie currently works for NSW Health in the training and education of health staff.

Lee Cheng Koay holds a Master of Crosscultural and Applied Linguistics and a Master of Health Communication. With a background in educational writing and health communication, Lee Cheng is currently conducting her PhD studies to integrate CREDIBLE into the development of a health campaign, specifically on endometriosis in Malaysia.

From left to right: Aurelie Mallet, Lee Cheng Koay, and Ahmar Mahboob

Subaltern Linguistics

A Toolkit for Alternative Education and Practice

Ahmar Mahboob,
Aurelie Mallet, and
Lee Cheng Koay

LONDON AND NEW YORK

First published 2025
by Routledge
4 Park Square, Milton Park, Abingdon, Oxon OX14 4RN

and by Routledge
605 Third Avenue, New York, NY 10158

Routledge is an imprint of the Taylor & Francis Group, an informa business

© 2025 Ahmar Mahboob, Aurelie Mallet, and Lee Cheng Koay

The right of Ahmar Mahboob, Aurelie Mallet, and Lee Cheng Koay to be identified as authors of this work has been asserted in accordance with sections 77 and 78 of the Copyright, Designs and Patents Act 1988.

All rights reserved. No part of this book may be reprinted or reproduced or utilised in any form or by any electronic, mechanical, or other means, now known or hereafter invented, including photocopying and recording, or in any information storage or retrieval system, without permission in writing from the publishers.

Trademark notice: Product or corporate names may be trademarks or registered trademarks, and are used only for identification and explanation without intent to infringe.

British Library Cataloguing-in-Publication Data
A catalogue record for this book is available from the British Library

ISBN: 9781032800301 (hbk)
ISBN: 9781032800325 (pbk)
ISBN: 9781003495086 (ebk)

DOI: 10.4324/9781003495086

Typeset in Sabon
by Newgen Publishing UK

Access the Support Material: www.routledge.com/9781032800325

To the victims of colonial violence, including material-biological and socio-semiotic violence

Contents

Acknowledgements   ix

Part I: Why do we need CREDIBLE projects?   1

1 Introduction   3

2 Making sense of the world   13

3 Moving forward with practice   30

Part II: What are CREDIBLE projects?   43

4 CREDIBLE projects for education   45

5 CREDIBLE projects for the environment   59

6 CREDIBLE projects for health and wellbeing   66

7 CREDIBLE projects for economic development   74

Part III: How to create CREDIBLE projects   83

8 How do we do CREDIBLE? – *The Ribbit-Ribbit Pond*   85

9 Let's do CREDIBLE together – taking care of the environment   102

10 It's now your turn to do CREDIBLE!   114

Part IV: Examples of CREDIBLE projects   **121**

11 Kids Guide to Art in Camden – mapping art spaces
    and places   123

12 Cards for Courage   136

13 Gender stereotypes in fairy tales: the CREDIBLE Project's
    journey of designing a workshop   151

14 Cantonese dialect maintenance among children   177

Index   188

Acknowledgements

Subaltern linguistics and practice, which is operationalised through the CREDIBLE approach, has developed over years in some of the units included in the Masters program in Crosscultural and Applied Linguistics at the University of Sydney. In specific, students enrolled in Sunny Boy's units (including, but not restricted to LNGS 7002, Language, Society, and Power; LNGS 7102, Educational Linguistics; and LNGS 7501, Professional Practice) have been creating CREDIBLE projects for the last five years or so, with support from Aurelie and Lee Cheng. This work has enabled us to develop teaching tools, strategies, and material that works well for the students – the success of this work is best evaluated by looking at the projects and outcomes of the work carried out by our students. This book is primarily based on the material that we first developed for these students and courses. So, first, we would like to acknowledge all our students, their energy, engagement, and creativity. Without them, this book and our work would not be possible. In particular, we would like to thank Kiyara Grenfell, Syeda Sughra Naqvi, Jingchen Shi, Xinyan Wang, Yue Shu, Elisa Ueno, Indiana Salsabila, Qi Wang, Wenrui Zhang, Jianying Huang, Qintang Yu, and Mengling Zhao for giving us permission to use their reports in Part IV of the book.

In addition to students at USYD, we have been working with colleagues and students across many parts of the world to create and enable CREDIBLE projects. Their work, some of which is included in this book, has been instrumental in drafting a book that can work across different contexts and regions. We acknowledge all of them, even if we have not named them here – this is because there are so many of you and we don't want to leave out any one by naming a few people. You know who you are, and we love and appreciate your support, encouragement, and engagement.

The goal of the CREDIBLE approach is to enable participants to create economies, practices, projects, and resources to develop and promote community beneficial socio-semiotic processes in their own contexts. As such, this book is designed to support others in their initiatives. We acknowledge you – the readers and users of this book – for taking on the challenge and finding ways in which you can support the needs of your own communities – and, by doing so, support all of us.

Finally, we would like to thank the anonymous reviewers of this book, our colleagues who have endorsed this book, and the commissioning editor and production team at Routledge who helped to get this book to you.

Thank you all ♡
Sunny Boy, Aurelie, and Lee Cheng

Part I
Why do we need CREDIBLE projects?

Part I of the book establishes the urgency of developing practices that provide alternatives to colonial and coloniality-enabling research and teaching practices.

Chapter 1 starts out with a critique of using literacy as a key tool for evaluating individuals (and communities) and challenges theorisations of language as carried out in and through English. As an alternative, the chapter uses the concept of 'boli' in understanding and theorising speech (as distinct from reading/writing).

Chapter 2 then encourages us to rethink our primary assumptions about knowledge and meaning making. In doing this, we look at how we draw on all our sensory systems in understanding and engaging with the world around us and how these systems operate by creating symbolic relationships.

Building on the first two chapters, Chapter 3 introduces the CREDIBLE approach as a framework to create alternative approaches to education and research. This chapter includes four examples from real-world settings which were developed independent of our work. These examples show how CREDIBLE projects are already carried out and how we can learn from them to develop our own work.

1 Introduction

Auntie Brumby survived the colonial onslaught against her and Mother Earth that has led to innumerable species extinction and pollution of our mind, air, water, and land. And if we listen to her words, we can learn to survive as well – and, perhaps, even to find solutions to some of the problems.

> *"Come heeeere, Sunny Boy", Auntie Brumby called,*
> *"You are a pony now; but you need to start learning*
> *That not all you see or hear is true*
> *Specially, don't trust sounds and scribbles,*
> *Without seeing action, action, and more action."*
>
> *"Sounds and scribbles make a magical charm*
> *Promising you everything and more*
> *Promising to fulfil your childhood dreams -*
> *Promises that are forgotten*
> *Before they are even made."*
>
> *"Come clooooser, Sunny Boy,*
> *Don't give your reins to anyone else*
> *They will steer you where they want to go*
> *Let you do all the hard work*
> *And then kick you when done."*
> *How did Auntie Brumby know*
> *That I just lost my hay*
> *And got nothing in return?*
> *Auntie Brumby knows all!*
>
> *Sunny Boy Brumby*

Auntie Brumby is wise in recognising that modern-colonial education, which is grounded in reading/writing (basic literacy), often requires one to build beliefs on unobservable and unverifiable abstract knowledge that is prescribed through curricula and media. Success in schools is achieved by demonstrating that one has accepted and internalised required information and practices. In accepting reading (and other media) as a dominant source of beliefs and knowledge formation, one puts one's trust in the people responsible for the design, development, and delivery of that material. This is a highly risky thing to do because those who design, develop, and deliver education have their own interests and goals that they want to achieve. And, in the context of dominant forms of education and knowledge today, the designers and developers of education tend to be those associated with colonial and coloniality-enabling agendas. This is part of the reason why schools today fail to enable students to become independent and participatory citizens. Instead, school knowledge and training enable one to seek employment and earn one's means of existence by working for others.

To redress the harm done by colonial and/or coloniality-enabling education, we need educational practices that aim to enable students to create things, including material, resources, and economies to address real-world issues in their contexts. This book shares one attempt that we have been developing and piloting with our students and colleagues in different parts of the world. The goal of the CREDIBLE approach, which is an example of subaltern practice, is to enable participants to create economies, practices, projects, and resources to develop and promote community beneficial socio-semiotic processes in their own language (or a language of their choice). Socio-semiotics, which we will discuss in more detail in Chapter 2, can broadly be understood as ways in which various meaning-making resources (including, but not limited to, images, texts, colours, gestures, movement, sounds, smells, tastes, and touch) relate to the lives of people.

This book, divided into four parts, showcases how a CREDIBLE approach to research and education can be carried out and how it serves as an example of subaltern linguistics and practice. Part I shares the reasons we need to consider alternative approaches to education, linguistics, and research. We introduce some key concepts that the CREDIBLE approach draws on as well as describe what CREDIBLE projects are and can look like. This section includes three chapters. In Chapter 1, after this brief intro, we will investigate ways in which colonisation continues today through academia and education, with a focus on how literacy is exploited for these purposes. Chapter 2 attempts to provide an alternative way of making sense of the world around us that does not fall for colonial-era human-centric beliefs and practices. Chapter 3 then draws on this framework to outline how we can set up CREDIBLE projects and practices.

In Part II we share what can be done when we adopt a CREDIBLE and subaltern approach. This part includes several examples of student projects across a range of areas including education, environment, healthcare, and economy. Part III of the book provides detailed guidelines and instructions on how to develop CREDIBLE projects. We include worksheets and activities that can be used to conceptualise, plan, and develop CREDIBLE projects. And, in Part IV of the book, we include four examples of students' CREDIBLE project reports. In addition to serving as additional examples, they also illustrate how CREDIBLE projects can be written up for wider dissemination.

The myth of the post-colonial

A people cannot be post-colonial until their ways of knowing, being, and doing are independent of colonial influences. European colonisers, during their occupation, first dispossessed the Indigenous populations of their rights, wealth, knowledge, and wisdom; and then replaced these with colonial laws, economies, and education. Since colonial socio-semiotics continue to dominate today, there is little reason to think that we live in a post-colonial world. A larger proportion of the human population is colonised today than it was during the heyday of the traditional period of colonisation. And, in addition to the Anglo-European colonial masters, there are multiple layers of other/local colonisers and masters.

> They took away my land, I said:
> Thank you for building the railroad.
>
> They took away my wealth, I said:
> Thank you for giving me loans.
>
> They took away my language, I said:
> Thank you for teaching me to speak.
>
> They took away my traditions, I said:
> Thank you for giving me culture.
>
> They took away my wisdom, I said:
> Thank you for building us schools.
>
> They took away my values, I said:
> Thank you for making me civilised.
>
> They took away my honour, I said:
> Thank you for being so kind.
>
> They took away my people, I said:
> Thank you for giving us jobs.

> They took away my life, I said:
> Thank you for teaching me to live.
>
> Ahmar Mahboob

Colonisation today is grounded in the subservience of our socio-semiotic systems (ways of being, knowing, and doing) to our colonisers (this may include layers of global and/or local colonisers). We can observe this in the fractals of oppression around the world: those dominated often dominate in turn. From a handful of people who manage most of the resources of the world to a child bullied into submission in school – there is a pattern of suppression/oppression that is indicative and constitutive of the oppressive world that many of us live in. Very few are free of such oppression. However, these fractals, as fractals in any complex dynamic system, are always unstable and can change. And these changes may be triggered by creating and practicing alternatives approaches to colonial academia and knowledge-making.

This book provides one example of an alternative approach to research and education that we have been trying out. However, before we introduce our work in more detail, we will discuss one key problem with education that enables the colonisation of our minds: the use of literacy (reading/writing) as the primary vehicle for content delivery and for assessment.

The problems with literacy as the goal of education

Literacy, in a traditional view, is seen as the ability to read and write. A key goal of modern education is to teach students to read and write and then assess them on their ability to remember bits of information. Current assessment practices evaluate an individual's grasp of literacy practices and opens or closes life opportunities for each person based on their performance on specified tests and assessments. Those who succeed in demonstrating skills and ability in an 'other' defined set of literacy practices may be given options to progress and get employed by local/foreign corporations. In doing so, dominant forms of education – with literacy development as their goal – enable the conditions that allow the elites to retain their power and authority.

The problem with literacy, it needs to be stressed, is NOT with its use of one form of visual symbols to develop, share, or preserve meanings. The problem with literacy is in its use as a key measurement of education and ability – people with low or no literacy, one will observe, are discriminated against in most contexts.

Literacy, it needs to be noted, is not primary to human learning and development. If it were, all human communities would have evolved literacy for this purpose. Observation tells us that most Indigenous communities did not use literacy for education. This does not mean that communities around the world did not have literacy before modern education: literacy evolved and was used by different groups of people for different purposes at various times in history. However, literacy was not used as the dominant medium of education and assessment across the world.

In contrast, all humans – like other biological species – primarily use non-literacy-based forms of communication and engagement. For humans, regardless of their location, speech, or 'boli', as it is lexicalised in Sunny Boy's speech, is a shared resource for meaning making and communicating.

Technicalising 'boli' as subaltern linguistics and practice

Boli (speech) is dynamic: she (yes, boli has a gender in Sunny Boy's boli ☺) represents, informs, responds to, and evolves in relation to the needs and geographical contexts of her users. Boli shifts and changes continuously. Boli is a socio-semiotic inheritance we receive from our ancestors (this can be contrasted with DNA, which is our biological inheritance). Boli is not restricted to humans: non-humans also have boli, e.g. 'bakri ki boli' (a goat's boli), 'chirya ki boli' (a bird's boli). While there is little evidence to claim that other species and life forms use the limited range of sounds humans use to interact; there is plenty of evidence that shows that different species use other sound frequencies and/or sensory systems to create and enact their socio-semiotics.

Boli was the primary medium of education in pre-colonial South Asia, as in most parts of the world before European colonisation and modern education. Literacy existed in many places and at different periods in time. However, it was primarily used by the trading classes, who needed it for record keeping and other trading needs. Other communities (many of whom were nomadic and lived across vast regions) did not have a need for literacy, and hence did not develop it.

Pre-colonial South Asia used boli as the primary modality for education. Education was based on an apprenticeship model, not literacy. Students learnt by observing, listening, and participating. While most traditional forms of education have been dismantled across South Asia in favour of literacy-based models marketed by exploitative powers, we still find some remnants of this practice in certain professions. For example, even today, if one wants to learn music in South Asia, one becomes an apprentice and learns from an 'Ustad' (an expert performer and teacher). The same practice of apprenticeship also operates in most unregulated local industries, such as auto-mechanic work, plumbing, and carpentry across the region.

Education in the pre-colonial period was designed to serve the needs of the people. Through education, one developed ability (not literacy) in areas needed for the well-being of the community. This required education to be based on understandings of the local context and needs, not necessarily texts written in (or translated from) foreign languages, which are often reflective of different socio-cultural and geographical settings. In addition, skills were distributed in a community, where people apprenticed – either formally or informally – and developed skills in areas where they excelled.

As we now also know from academic work, intelligences are multiple and different people have different things that they are better at. For example, Sunny Boy claims he would be terrible at most sports, partly because he lacks the kind of skills and intelligence needed to be good at sports. Literacy, if it did exist in a community, for example the trading communities, would be passed on to those who took interest in it. For others, there were plenty of other things that they could do and contribute towards. Literacy was not needed for such a distribution of skills and forms of education.

A required use of literacy in education leads to a number of problems. For example, the content and language of educational material can become a major problem. Educational material can be biased and/or false (fake news) and is written by and in the interest of the dominant powers (locally, regionally, and/or internationally). One implication of this observation, which can be verified by reading through textbooks (e.g. those used in Pakistani schools), is that we need to learn and teach to question almost everything that is normalised through colonial models of education, literacy, and knowledge production.

Taking boli as a starting point, instead of 'language', leads us to understandings that are quite different from those promoted in English-based linguistics. For example, the concept of boli, which is only oral, does not conflate two different sensory systems: sound and sight. Boli operates through sound only; writing systems are not required for a boli. This contrasts with the English notion of a language, which includes two modes: speech and writing. In English, writing is given the same importance as oral language; and, in exploitative education, reading/writing is given more importance than listening-speaking, e.g., formal and summative assessments tend to be literacy-based. This leads to marginalisation of people from under-privileged and no/low-literacy backgrounds.

Current educational and other policies do not recognise boli that do not have a writing system – so, for many people around the world, their boli is invisible from education, governance, economy, law, and other domains of life. This leads to people dropping their boli for a more powerful 'language'. And, with that shift, boli – the socio-semiotic inheritance and a repository of local knowledge and science – starts to wane and potentially die out. While linguists and others regret the loss of boli, nothing substantial is done to support the well-being of the people who speak/spoke this boli. It is ironic that colonial linguists tend to forget that it is not the boli that suffers, it is people who speak the boli who are suffering. Instead of just documenting boli, our work needs to support the people. If the people are well and strong, they will have a strong boli; if the people are weak and defeated, their boli will deteriorate too.

On a different but related note, we need to recognise that most new writing systems promoted by colonial or coloniality-enabling linguists are phonetic (i.e., characters represent individual sounds, as in English). Phonetic writing systems, as will be discussed next, are amongst the worst forms of writing systems. To understand this, we need to understand what writing systems are and how they operate.

From boli to writing systems

Writing systems use visual symbols used to create and represent meanings or sounds. As such, visual symbols can be independent of sounds. A purely visual writing system would carry meaning without any correlation with sound. Observe that the only extant writing system that does so to a degree is Chinese. All other writing systems use symbols that denote individual sounds or a combination of sounds. Amongst these, some writing systems use symbols for a syllable (e.g. Cherokee, Katakana, and pre-colonial Indigenous languages across many parts of Southeast Asia), while others use symbols to mark phonetic contrasts (e.g. English, Arabic, and almost all scripts created by modern linguists).

Syllable-based writings systems, because they focus on syllables and not individual sounds, can accommodate a larger variation of accents and dialects. It is noteworthy that the colonial/occupying western European colonial powers systematically replaced the syllabic writing systems with phonetic ones. This is part of the socio-semiotic violence that they carried out against Indigenous communities. For example, the Sasak language used in Lombok, Indonensia, had an Indigenous syllabic writing system (see Figure 1.1). This system was replaced by a colonial-inspired phonetic writing system which is arguably not as good as the Indigenous one.

In contrast to syllabic writing systems, phonetic scripts are highly sensitive to variations in peoples' dialects, sociolects, and idiolects. This is one reason that people spell the same words in different ways based on the dialect they speak. One job of literacy-based education is to suppress these deviations and variations; literacy-based education promotes and evaluates people based on pre-defined sets of spellings, words, and grammars. Deviations to expected norms are often marked

Figure 1.1 A collection of ancient Sasak Aksaara texts from Lombok carved on Lontar Leaves. Picture taken in mid-2024 by Raden Prawangsa Jaya Ningrat, a custodian and manager of the Sasak traditions and culture. [Note: we requested Raden to send us a close-up picture of one of the precious texts and he replied, "I have to find a special time to take pictures because not everyone present is allowed for this activity" which signifies the respect that is given to these texts by the community.]

as mistakes and errors and looked down upon. Evidence for this can be found by looking at feedback given to students' from almost any part of the world.

Another issue with literacy is that it attempts to restrain and 'standardise' a system that is inherently dynamic. Trying to restrain the dynamicity of boli or oral language through the adoption of one (or selected) forms of 'language', 'grammar', and 'literacy' disempowers people who do not come from certain backgrounds. Literacy also restricts what people are allowed to *do* with language and how. The restrictions imposed on language and literacy in exploitative education impact what and how people learn. In many parts of the world, students learn stuff that is not directly relevant to their local needs and context and is not designed to enable people to meet their needs or enable local economies and initiatives.

Boli, as we have mentioned before, is a socio-semiotic inheritance. Boli is learnt from one's caretakers and encapsulates the essence of what ones' ancestors learnt about and from their environment; along with information about what to do, how, when, where, why, and with whom. This local and contextual learning, which is encapsulated in boli, evolves over generations in geographical regions and is passed on from one generation to the next. In many ways, boli is a socio-semiotic inheritance that we receive from our ancestors – and can be compared to DNA, which is our biological inheritance. Notice how, when we deny other people's boli, we deny them the right to use and benefit from their socio-semiotic inheritance. By replacing local and Indigenous boli with non-local languages, education in most exploited locations has and continues to destroy Indigenous and local knowledges, sciences, and peoples.

Boli is science

How is a replacement of boli a destruction of local science? To understand this, we need to first understand what science is. At the most fundamental level, without methodologies and applications, science is a way of sorting things, i.e., of categorising or classifying things. All boli sort the world around them, i.e., they create taxonomies. And, in doing so, they show us how boli is the fundamental of all sciences. Furthermore, each boli carves up the world in a slightly different way: this is observed in the variations in meanings and things that boli represent and do. Boli, in a nutshell, is its own science: it presents a unique and geographically embedded way of seeing and understanding the world; and, in extension, relating to that world. One reason why a variety of boli or languages are different from each other – and some have wider currency than others – is because of the way they are spread across different geographical settings/range and across varying human populations.

One reason why English is the language of global dominance is that the English empire controlled very large parts of the world, forced their language and practices on the local populations, and integrated terms and concepts from those places into the English language. At the same time, they encouraged the borrowing of English terms and concepts into boli. The English rewarded locals who learnt their language and ways by giving them jobs, resources, and prestige – not unlike what English offers to many today. By doing so, English language and English ways of knowing and doing are given preference over other languages and ways – and, slowly, the local populations, their ways of knowing, of being, and of supporting local communities, economies, and ecologies are lost and/or replaced. And this loss of our socio-semiotic inheritance, coupled with economic, social, and political suppression, contribute to ecological, social, and political disasters.

From a critique of literacy to having no references

In recognition of the problems with literacy-based work, we have not included any references in this book. This does not imply that we have not read or appreciate the work of others on this and similar issues. We are aware that there is a long tradition of work that addresses issues of inequality in education and society. This includes work across a range of disciplines and sub-disciplines. We are familiar with some of this work and recognise its influence on our work and writing. At the same time, with due apology, we have chosen not to include references in this book (other than references included by students in their CREDIBLE reports).

We did this for several reasons. First, we asked ourselves these two interrelated questions: 1) how can we model subaltern linguistics and practice if we continue to replicate approaches that are dominant in the work that we are critiquing; and 2) when references are often used to enable silos and silence dissent, should we use them in subaltern work?

In addition, five additional interrelated reasons led us into deciding to exclude references in this book:

- References have to be trusted, as not everyone has or can do the same readings (and with the same interpretations);
- References relate to other written texts (often in English), which exclude other forms of knowledge (specially in boli that don't have a writing system or don't use it in academia);
- Selecting references can be a political act through which certain people and work are promoted and others dismissed;
- References, when used instead of observations/evidence to make/support a point, must be taken at face-value as there is little that readers can do to verify them; and,
- References can make reading difficult, especially for those uninitiated in the field.

While we acknowledge and respect other people's work and contributions, we have chosen not to include direct references in most parts of this book (Part IV of the book is an exception because it includes student project reports that included references). We apologise to those who might be impacted by this choice.

In this book, we have shared our observations and/or pointed to things that you can locate and observe yourselves; and, we have included poems and images that encourage one to reflect on the same issues in a different way. By doing so, in many ways, we are delegating the authority and expertise typically reserved for 'the author' to you, the reader: we have shared examples and observations, and you have the agency to verify them – our arguments are not protected by a ($$$) reference-wall.

Moving forward…

In this chapter, we problematised the dominance of literacy (reading/writing) in education and evaluation. Having done so, we need to create alternative ways of understanding and engaging with the world around us. Chapter 2 shares one way that we have found useful, and which can translate into practice (focus of Chapter 3 and the rest of the book).

2 Making sense of the world

Like computer languages program machines,
Human language programs people;
And while we do have other senses,
Language can shape how we use those too.

Language co-evolved with where she grew:
With lands, creatures, and seasons she knew.
Our elders learned all that was needed
And taught it to us through *boli* and practice:

The flow of sounds, the melodies of song
The rhythm of knowledge, the grammars of dance
The meaning of colours, the semantics of smell
The discourse of touch, the sense of flavours

A harmonic system in a mystical garden.

All that changed when our tongue was cut:
Our laws replaced by foreign words
Our knowledge drowned in information floods
Our wisdom stolen through tests and books
Our traditions slaughtered by trends and fads
Our integrity replaced with wants and greed
Our humanity turned into an infectious wound

An agitated system in a turbulent existence.

Prof Nomad

Prof Nomad's poem captures some of the key ideas shared in Chapter 1. It also focuses on how Indigenous education was grounded in boli (speech) and practice, which incorporated all sensory systems and their uses in a range of formats and modes. In boli, speech is never confused or conflated with 'likhai' (writing), which is recognised as an independent and learnt skill: it is not an innate human ability. The use of literacy as

DOI: 10.4324/9781003495086-3

Figure 2.1 Image of 'The black stone' taken by Sunny Boy at the University of St Andrews in Scotland, UK, in early 2023

Description reads:

"Testing times!

From the 1400s to 1700s students had oral exams. Sitting on this cold stone, they were questioned by their teachers.

In the modern university most examinations are written. All the students in a hall, pouring their knowledge onto paper, watching the ticking clock.

The hard work over, students enjoy that final University rite of passage, graduation.

The black stone

A solid block of granite used as a seat in exams from about 1420.

Exam hall clock

Made by G. Munro, 1930, St Andrews (Scotland)"

the key vehicle of education and evaluation for all is unfair and exploitative because it is based on an ability that is not innate to humans.

While a world without literacy-focused education might be hard to imagine for many today, literacy was introduced as the main vehicle of education and assessment in the late 18th / early 19th century – and that too in elite and privileged institutions (as evidence, see Figure 2.1). The use of literacy for public/mass education came much later in 19th century; and, for most colonial subjects in the 20th century: it was introduced and enforced during colonisation as a tool to build and maintain colonial hegemonies.

The use of literacy in education was preferred by the colonisers because of its effective use during the Reformation in 16th century western Europe which exploited the redesigned printing press (it was not a 'new' invention) to spread influence. Published material, as discussed in Chapter 1, refers to things that are typically not in the immediate environment of the reader and are often not directly observable or verifiable. By publishing books and material to be used as primary sources in pretty much all of academia, the colonials shaped how dominant approaches to knowledge and knowledge production operate today: to build beliefs and knowledge based on media (which includes but is not limited to books) rather than observation and engagement.

Subaltern linguistics and practice is an attempt to share alternative ways of doing research and education that support local needs rather than colonial and corporate interests. To develop this work, we need to first consider two things:

1. We need to consider how knowledge is made;
2. We need to consider how we make sense of the world.

What is knowledge?

Knowledge is one way in which living creatures make sense and engage with the world around them. As such, knowledge is infinite – it has no bounds. And, while we recognise that some knowledge and forms of knowledge are more applicable in some contexts than others, knowledge itself cannot be ranked (since it is infinite). Until recently, most humans had a relatively limited geographical range and knew most about the lands where they lived and moved about. This knowledge was thus geographically bound and quite distinct from each other. During colonisation, these local epistemologies (ways of knowing, doing, and being) were ridiculed and demonised as folk science or superstition and colonial sciences were recognised as the only legitimate sciences.

To better understand how knowledge is infinite, we can carry out a little activity:

> Take a bucket and put about 100 random objects in it. It doesn't matter what the objects are as long as they are all different. Now, spread them out on the floor and sort them. It doesn't matter how you sort them; there is no right or wrong way.
>
> Good☺
>
> Now, jumble everything up and then sort the stuff again.
>
> Now, jumble up everything once more and ask someone else (who has not seen you do this) to sort the stuff out. Tell them what we told you: they can do it any way they like, there is no right or wrong way.
>
> The chances are:
>
> - Each time you sorted the items, you did it differently; and,
> - The other person sorted the things differently from you.
>
> Congratulations! You have just become knowledge makers☺

What you just did is to categorise things. Making categories and classifying things is doing fundamental science, stripped of all its methodologies, approaches, and applications. Or, in other words, sorting is the first step of knowledge-making.

Notice that every time we sort a bucket of finite stuff, we tend to do it differently. When different people do it, they often do it differently. We sort based on our own choices, interests, experiences, thoughts, abilities, beliefs, moods…

Now, imagine, an infinite number of things. Would there not be an infinite number of ways that we can sort them? These will be based on what we want to do with the sorting, where, when, how, and with whom we are sorting. Changing any of these (or other) variables can change our sorting. And, changing the way we sort can change the outcomes and applications of what we do with the sorting.

This is one reason why people have different languages in different parts of the world: amongst other things, boli names and sorts out stuff which enables people to engage with each other and the world. Through this sorting, they create knowledge that connects them to the physical world around them. Thus, in its core, language and science are the same things.

If we remove a person who speaks X boli and place them, say, 5000 km away from where their boli evolved, they may not be able to use their boli to understand many/most things that they see around them: boli, and the science that it carries, is geographically bound. This explains why English and other languages used across large geographical regions appear to be more *developed* in their ability to describe and theorise: they are based on a broader range of experiences and information. At the same time, damaging or replacing Indigenous languages/sciences with English or another non-Indigenous boli/science can lead to environmental catastrophe. Damaging eco-linguistic environments brings the same types of destruction to humans as destroying eco-biological environments brings to other creatures: oppression and loss.

Since each boli sorts the world in a different way, colonial languages and forms of knowledge and knowledge building represent only a fraction of the ways in which knowledge can be built. Mostly, this knowledge structure denigrates Indigenous sciences. And, as we will demonstrate in this chapter, colonial-established forms of knowledge building are not necessarily a good way of doing knowledge building.

Why?

Because colonial-era disciplines (pretty much all of them) build categories in two primary ways:

1) Through structural/functional analysis (e.g., grammatical patterns); and
2) Through genealogy (e.g., genus, species, family).

Colonial sciences use structural/functional analysis to make arguments for the genealogical relationships between things. This is why species can get reclassified based on DNA evidence; or a boli can be put into another family based on new structural/functional analyses.

While using structures/functions is one way of sorting, there can be other ways of classifying things too. For example, one can sort based on inter-relationships, inter-dependencies, and/or co-existence – approaches espoused by many Indigenous communities world-wide. In creating such knowledge, structural/functional differences would not always be relevant or important. And, thus, both the knowledge we create and the benefits we get from it will be different.

Using structures/functions to support arguments of genealogy, on the other hand, contributes to creating a classification system that divides entities based on a few human-identified features; ignoring their co-existence and their inter-relationships. A structural/functional classificatory system, by its very nature, is divisive.

When considered in relation to different sciences, a genealogical and structural/functional approach produces studies that divide things up, e.g. in biology and linguistics, people look at genealogical relationships between species or languages. And, because division is an infinite act (one can keep on dividing and dividing), colonial sciences keep getting more and more delicate in their study; or, in other words, they split hairs. This is one reason why western academia often recategorises things and/or creates new categories. As their perspectives on things shift, based on various reasons (including socio-political ones), so do their categories and classifications.

Now, consider another way of sorting out the world: categorise things as 'infinite' and 'finite'. Infinite things are things that have no bounds: e.g., knowledge, money, power, faith, belief, numbers…; and finite things are things that are limited: e.g. trees, water, species, matter, life…

Once we do this, we can begin to realise that if we set anything in the 'infinite' category as our goal, we are setting ourselves up for failure.

Why?

Because something that is infinite can never be achieved: it is endless.

By splitting hairs, colonial sciences, education, and models of development have set their goal to be the 'infinite'. And, by doing so, they have set an unachievable goal. A goal that is, by definition, meant to fail.

Colonial sciences use finite resources to try to conquer the infinite: e.g., scientists burn incredibly large amounts of matter, which humans cannot replace/remake, to reach out into the infinite space. One doesn't need to be a rocket scientist (pun intended) to realise that one will run out of finite resources but never achieve the infinite.

Would it not make sense to use the infinite as a resource to learn about and contribute to the finite? That is, do something which is theoretically plausible.

Using 'finite' and 'infinite' is also just another way of carving up the world. There are many other ways of categorising the world around us. Some are good for one purpose, others are good for a different purpose; some categories explain only a few things, others can explain many more things; and some ways of creating categories can harmonise the world, and others can disharmonise it.

Setting items in the infinite category, such as seeking knowledge, as our goals can lead to disharmonisation because we are setting unachievable goals. In addition, the principles of sorting on which colonial knowledge making are based are inherently divisive and destructive: they are designed to benefit the colonisers. This is one reason why we keep producing *knowledge*, but the world keeps getting observably and experientially worse off.

To remedy the mess that colonial sciences and education have created, we need to reset our goals to 'finite' things and use the 'infinite' as resources. Once we do this, we will start to see a reharmonisation of the finite; and, luckily, we will have the infinite to help us out with what we need.

Making sense of the world

The world around us is made of physical-biological entities. In addition, we also know that there is a world that is non-material: a world full of ideas, and thoughts, and feelings, and knowledge, and beliefs, and dreams, and questions. Let us call this the socio-semiotic world. A world which exists for each of us; but its existence is not material. Its existence is socio-semiotic: it evolves and exists in social contexts; and it can change or alter at any time for any reason.

From observation of other living beings, we can note that they all interact with others of their species as well as the environment around them. To do this, they need to make sense of the world and share their understandings with others of their kind. Given the differences between humans and other living things, it is not feasible for us to understand how they experience or make sense of life. In fact, in our experience of life, we know that we can't even really know what another person thinks and feels like.

Can you think like a duck?
"Look Papa", he said one day by the pond,
"From a distance they all look the same,
But when you come closer, you can tell the difference:
Some have spots over there,
And others here", as he pointed to a spot on his face.
"Do they have names for each other?"

"Look Papa", he observed,
"Why are some swimming this way
And others the other...
Look, this one was coming here
And now she is going over there.
I wonder how I can know if it's a she or a he?"

"Look, Papa", he pondered,
"They don't make sense:
Dodo here, he was with that group here;
And Didi over there, with the others...
And now the two are together over there.
I just can't think like a duck, Papa."

I can't either Guddu. Let me ask if others can:
Can you think like a duck?

Ahmar Mahboob

Two worlds

We note that in studying material-biological sciences, people tend to agree upon the use of the *atom* as the smallest unit of matter (although it can also be spilt further). And, based on an agreed set of assumptions, material-biological scientists develop and use different methodologies and approaches in doing something to manipulate *atoms* to achieve their goals. In contrast, people who study social sciences do not currently have a unified approach. Instead, they study each subject area within social sciences differently. This implies that there is little consensus between people about the nature and substance of social sciences; and this leads to different disciplines and specialists doing their own things. However, this can change if we consider *symbols* (or symbolic relationships) as the central building block of our socio-semiotic worlds.

We live in both the material-biological and socio-semiotic worlds simultaneously. The material-biological world is comprised of atoms just as the socio-semiotic world is constructed through symbolic relationships. Symbols are used across all our sensory and socio-semiotic systems to create and exchange meanings. For example, in economics, money is a symbol; in mathematics, numbers and signs are symbols; in linguistics, sounds and scribblings are symbols; in religious studies, various objects and practices can take on symbolic meanings.

The material-biological and socio-semiotic worlds interact in and through each one of us – individually and collectively. Table 2.1 sets out some of the key differences between these two worlds.

Table 2.1 Some key differences between the material-biological and socio-semiotic worlds

Material-biological world	Socio-semiotic world
Made of matter: it has physical existence	Not made of matter: it does not have physical existence
Comprised of particles, called *atoms*	Comprised of non-particles, called *symbols*
Material particles interact with each other based on physical properties	Non-material particles are placed into patterns
May exist without socio-semiotics	Does not exist without the material-biological
Existence may or may not be dependent on humans	Existence is dependent on our existence
Material force required to make changes	Material force is not essential to make changes
Changes are influenced by principles of the material-biological world	Changes can occur at any time and for any reason
Mathematics can be used to study them	Mathematics does not operate
Studied in disciplines such as physics, chemistry, biology…	Studied in disciplines such as sociology, linguistics, economics, religious studies…

Before discussing the differences between the material-biological and socio-semiotic worlds (Table 2.1), let us briefly discuss why we have not separated out material and biological entities.

The primary reason for putting material-biological into a single category is that we do not have a viable definition of 'life'. And, without it, we cannot really identify what is alive and what is not. The problem here is very similar to that in linguistics: biologists have established a discipline where they claim to study life without defining 'life'. Instead, just like linguists create the discipline of 'linguistics' by contrasting human language and non-human communication, biologists create the discipline of 'biology' by listing a set of characteristics that they consider as differences between living and non-living things (e.g., reproduction, growth). It is also noteworthy that biologists tend to discount any counter evidence. For example, 'trovants', a kind of rock found in certain parts of the world, have been documented to grow, move, and reproduce. Scientists are quick to explain that this is because of certain chemical reactions and not because the rocks are alive; but, is not all life based on some kinds of chemical reactions? In Indigenous cultures, Earth herself is alive; not just some things that exist on earth (and are made of/from earth). This difference of socio-semiotics between the colonial and Indigenous peoples partly explains the relationship that the two had with earth and nature (note: for Indigenous peoples, humans are part of nature, not above/outside it).

The material-biological world and the socio-semiotic worlds are quite distinct from each other even if they can impact each other. Our thoughts and beliefs can impact how we act and what we do. For example, if people think that trees and plants are not sentient, then they will be OK with cutting down forests; on the other hand, if people consider trees to have sentience – like most Indigenous peoples – then they will not. Similarly, our material-biological environments can impact how we see and engage with the world. For example, people who live in deserts and those who live in forests tend to have quite different ways in which they engage with their surroundings.

The material-biological world can exist without socio-semiotics because socio-semiotics exist as an ability of material-biological entities. Or, in other words, while the existence of material-biological entities may not be dependent on the existence of humans; human socio-semiotics cannot exist if humans don't exist. Changes in the material-biological world require physical force and are governed by the laws of nature, which can be studied mathematically. On the other hand, changes in our socio-semiotics can occur with or without the use of physical force. These changes can happen at any time and for any reason. In addition, since mathematics itself is a socio-semiotic creation, it does not apply to socio-semiotics. For example, while we can divide an apple into two halves, we cannot divide an idea into two halves. This observation has implications for social science research that is based on surveys and quantitative data. Since socio-semiotics may change at any time, a survey of attitudes and perceptions cannot be considered an accurate representation of people at any time other than when the data was collected (if that). This is partly why studies on attitudes and perceptions which are very common in academia tend not to have any real impact on our lives. To have impact, we need to create material-biological things that can alter attitudes.

For example, Ivan Gonzalez, the author of The Ribbit Ribbit Pond (www.flcgroup.net/ribbit-ribbit-pond/), which is described in more detail in Chapter 8 of this book, initially wanted to carry out a survey of attitudes towards migrants and refugees in Chile. After a discussion of how such a survey may give us some insights about what some people might think at a point in time but not have any real impact in terms of encouraging inclusivity in the community, we decided to create a children's story book that would encourage them to be more inclusive. The result of this work has not only had an impact in Ivan's immediate context, but the book took a life of its own and is currently available in 35 languages. These additional translations for the book were created by many collaborators who volunteered their time and energy because they liked the book and the message that the book carries. In this example, we can see how creating a material-biological object instead of carrying out a survey of socio-semiotic beliefs can make real-world impact. This is one reason why subaltern practice recommends that people create CREDIBLE projects instead of just carrying out theoretical and abstract studies.

In another example, discussed in more detail in Chapter 7 of this book, FLC in collaboration with the University of Malaya and the

Kristang community in Melaka, Malaysia, created a Language Travels project that enabled a micro-economy in and through the Kristang language instead of simply documenting the boli. We chose to create this project instead of documenting the boli because while a documentation of boli, which is typically carried out through colonial approaches to linguistics, may describe the grammar of a boli as used by some people in some contexts, it does not necessarily enable language maintenance. Language Travels, on the other hand, helps generate an income for the community and motivates the community to maintain their boli.

These projects exemplify how subaltern linguistics and practice, which is based on rethinking our understanding of and relationship with the world (instead of colonial knowledge and education), can help us to address real-world issues. To do this work, in addition to understanding the differences between the material-biological and socio-semiotic worlds, we also need to expand our understanding of how we make meaning and engage with the world with all the sensory systems that we have.

Sensory systems

Our only "real" access to the material world is through our material senses. Everything else, all manners in which we understand and share these understandings of the world are non-material. In addition, even things that are material for us are understood and interpreted differently by each individual and group. This is why nothing in human existence is static or constant: not even the human study of science or mathematics. While highly technicalised and internally consistent, the systems of science or mathematics, are not singular: there are multiple ways of doing what might be considered science or mathematics. Evidence of this, although fast disappearing, can still be found in the various Indigenous communities that have, e.g., different ways of counting and using colour terms.

As humans, we may use up to five sensory systems to make sense of the world. The sensory systems we have and how we use them varies across individuals and groups. Regardless of these variations, the sensory systems we have help us to interpret the different types of material stimulus (light, sound, smell, touch, and taste) in relation to our experiences, goals, and socio-semiotics. These sensory systems, it needs to be noted, are not totally independent of each other and often work together.

Table 2.2 provides an overview of how our material-biological self relates to our socio-semiotic self through our sensory systems. It shows how the five senses differ in terms of two features: distance/proximity to us; and ingestion (taking things inside our body). And it includes examples of how we experience and understand these. Note that all relationships between the material-biological world and the socio-semiotic world are symbolic and dynamic.

Table 2.2 Classification of human sensory systems

Sensory systems	(connect us to the physical-biological world, which is formed of atoms)			Human experiences (socio-semiotic world, which operates through symbols)
	Sense	Distance	Ingestion	
Group A (things may be in our presence or recorded)	Sight	+++	-	Literacy, movies...
	Sound	++	-	Boli, music...
Group B (things must be in our present)	Smell	+	+	Food, manure...
	Touch	0 / -	- / +	Braille, human...
	Taste	-	+	Food, flavour...

Group A sensory systems engage with things that are not ingested (while light and sound can penetrate our bodies, e.g. lasers, this is different from how our sensory systems draw on them); hence, they don't always need to be very close to us. We can see and hear things that are around us, at a distance from us, and those that have been recorded (e.g. through writing, art, audio/video recordings) or electronically/digitally transmitted (e.g., television, telephone, texting, radio, Zoom). In contrast, Group B sensory systems operate on things that can (and, in some cases, must) be ingested; hence, they must be in our present. For example, you may recall the smell, texture, and taste of the dinner you had at a dinner party last month, but you won't be able to smell, touch, or taste it at present. This is because we cannot smell, touch or taste things that are not in our present. Note also that things that we access through Group A senses can injure or hurt us, but they are unlikely to kill us (although it is possible through weapons that use light/sound). On the other hand, things that we access through Group B, have the potential of causing serious harm or of even killing us. This is partly why we can be fooled through sight/sound (especially by ones that are not present), but it is unlikely that we will want to touch or taste something if we don't feel comfortable with it in our present.

The sequencing of the sensory systems shared above can be understood in several ways. We will exemplify two here. Imagine that you see smoke rising from a forest in the distance. You will realise that there is a fire there but may not take any action. If you start to hear the fire, you will start getting worried as the fire is getting closer. If you start smelling smoke, you will start taking actions to protect yourself as the smoke signals that the fire is moving in your direction. If you start to feel the heat of the fire, you will be in panic and will need to take immediate action to protect yourself. And, if you can taste fire, you are in real danger and your life might be at risk.

Alternatively, imagine that you see people at a cafe. You recognise that these are other humans, but you don't really know them. If you start a conversation with them, you will start to get to know them better. Now, if you feel uncomfortable with how they smell, you will very likely move away. Otherwise, you may continue to engage with them, and the relationship might develop. Depending on the context, culture, and person, you may or may not touch them. Sharing touch says something about how close you are with them. And we share taste with people who are very close to or intimate with us. In many ways, our relationship with others can be understood in relation to how many senses we share with them. If we share all five senses, we have a closer relationship to them. This is one reason why a mother and baby have one of the strongest bonds. And, it also explains why, as a child grows older and shares fewer sensory systems with their mother, they become more independent and the relationship changes. In addition to the sensory systems, a sharing of socio-semiotics is also an indicator of how close we are to others. One of the strongest bonds between humans is where we share all our sensory systems as well as our socio-semiotics.

Sensory systems and education

Current colonial models of education are primarily dependent on Group A – formal school education happens through reading/writing (sight) and speech (sound). Relying solely on Group A sensory systems is a potential trap in education because things that we read and listen to may not be directly observable and hence not verifiable. For education to work through Group A only, we need to lower our guard and trust information given by others though various media and material. In other words, by accepting Group A based colonial knowledge, we are placing our trust into the people who built their knowledge and power by exploiting other humans, other life forms, and the environment.

In contrast, Indigenous and holistic approaches to education consider all five sensory experiences in thinking about education and training. Infants and children – in all parts of the world – start learning through Group B first. They learn through taste, touch, and smell before their eyesight and hearing is developed sufficiently to develop literacy or use boli. This is one reason why babies put pretty much anything they can get hold of in their mouths.

Schools today focus on literacy (sight) and oral teaching (sound); little attention, if any, is paid to other sensory systems or the interrelationship between the various sensory systems. For example, schools in Sunny Boy's city of birth can be over-crowded, dirty, smelly, and noisy: this impacts all aspects of the students' material-biological being and their socio-semiotic learning – but is disregarded by educational authorities, who focus on the curricula and tests/examinations. An over-emphasis on reading and a neglect of the local context and needs of the learners enables an educational system which situates students outside of their own contexts and does not help people address their own concerns and needs.

This removing of humans from their immediate contexts is a strategy used by colonial powers to influence individuals into acting in the interest of the colonials (and often against the interests of their own communities and environment). As people become more engaged in activities that are dependent on Group A of our material senses, i.e., senses that allow us to focus on things that are not in our present (or directly verifiable), we pay less attention to things that are closer to us and that we are surrounded by. By doing so, we can lose our connection with our material-biological surroundings and instead rally around things that only have a socio-semiotic (non-material) existence for most of us. We see evidence of this in how our educational system trains graduates who want to find jobs overseas to make some cash, instead of thinking about how they can improve the material situation in which they and their communities live. Similarly, we find that educational systems tend to teach and promote colonial and colonial-influenced histories that further divide the people and lead to conflict, violence, and poverty.

Most learning/teaching in colonial schools is based on textbooks and curricula that are controlled by governments. Often, as in the case of the development of the recent draft National Education Curriculum in Pakistan, there is no wider public consultation or engagement in the development of educational policies and material. The educational policies developed by various 'countries' are designed to aid in the economic progress of the country. To do this, the country prioritises content and goals that will lead to higher employment rates. As such, the educational policies of the colonised countries are ones that aim to aid economic development, which is managed by the colonial powers. And, while the policies might aim at economic development, a look around the world, especially in disempowered communities and countries, will show that it fails to achieve the desired results. Instead, we observe rates of unemployment and poverty rising, making these people/countries even more dependent on loans and other forms of aid and support.

Currently, education in the colonised communities is geared to serve the needs of elites and colonial masters, not the masses. In other words, the current educational system is designed to keep us colonised and subjugated rather than becoming independent and prosperous. This can be observed in how so many of our educational institutions pride themselves on having graduated students who have found jobs overseas, i.e., they have trained people who left their homes and communities in order to earn wages overseas (Ahmar recognises that they are one of those people who were expected to leave Pakistan, instead of staying there); and, hence, not trained people who stayed home and contributed to the betterment of local communities.

To move away from colonial control, we need an educational system that enables independence, instead of colonisation. An education that makes us independent is an education that:

a. is not consumed by the goal of spreading universal literacy;
b. is not designed to only prepare people to work for others for (petty) wages;
c. considers the needs of the community and then trains the citizens to learn to address those needs;
d. values all forms of knowledge and skills, not just ones included in colonial textbooks/languages;
e. is designed to make people able to manage their own needs and resources; and,
f. involves all stakeholders in its development and management.

If we are interested in creating such an education and practice, we need to support people, instead of constantly criticising them for not meeting colonial 'standards'. We also need to realise that wisdom and expertise comes through experience, engagement, and reflection, not by simply reading or being a critical thinker. Nor is knowledge restricted to English: boli is science, and this science is not restricted to English. Subaltern practice values expertise and practice, not the language it is in.

If we are interested in supporting people and environment through education, we need to reset the goals of education and focus on skills and practice rather than literacy. Skills, which require knowledge that can be orally (or visually, e.g. through drawing/animation) communicated and do NOT require literacy, can be used to make and do things: e.g., build systems and processes to manage air, water, and land pollution in our regions. These 'doings' can, in turn, help generate local economies and break the dependence on colonial knowledge and economy.

Giving skills, rather than focusing on literacy, requires an engagement with multiple material senses. Education practices that engage multiple material and non-material systems tend to be much more embedded within a community than those that engage with just a few. For example, an educational system that is mostly dependent on written texts may not be reflective of or relevant to people in different contexts. Since writing, a visual system, uses stimuli that are most distant from a person, it can also be difficult to ascertain the reliability and validity of the visual stimuli (e.g., most of the fake news on social media exploits our visual and auditory systems). While in some cases we can check to see if what we saw was right or wrong, e.g., if we see a potential threat in the distance, we can move closer to inspect it; in other cases, e.g. in the case of written texts, the referents are not necessarily accessible to us and cannot be verified. In such cases, if we believe the information we receive, then we are putting our trust in the source of the text.

And this is where potential problems lie. If the texts that students are exposed to in their education include lies and fake news, then students' socio-semiotics and their actions can be directed to achieve destructive goals. Unfortunately, at present, educational texts tend to be designed to engender the socio-semiotics of division and conflict and violence. That we find violence and poverty across many parts of the world should not come as a surprise – what we are seeing are the outcomes of the colonial education and literacy practices that we have now consumed for scores of generations and have internalised as 'facts'.

However, if we consider the non-material basis of these 'facts' and ask for material evidence to support them, we can start to unravel the threads that have kept us bound to colonial chains.

For example, as English language learners (and teachers/researchers) we learn and teach three tenses: past, present, and future. Now, instead of believing in the information as it is presented in textbooks, if we were to observe and analyse the English language, we would quickly note that while English does have a past tense, which is often marked by a slight sound change, it does NOT have a future tense. To refer to a future time in English, we use modals, e.g. will, shall, may, might. Notice that modality is not tense. Furthermore, in Sunny Boy's and Lee Cheng's boli there is no past tense either: we only have present tense because present is the only time one can observe and act in. So, then, one question that we can ask is: why are we taught (and in turn teach/research) tenses that don't exist?

Identifying and breaking the chains of socio-semiotic dependency is one key strategy to developing subaltern practice and education. In doing so, our goal is not to take our people/communities back-in-time, but rather to move forward with a shared vision of what we need to achieve. And, to achieve these goals, we will need to develop tools, strategies, and resources – using a range of material and non-material systems. In doing this, literacy can continue to play a role – but this use of literacy should be based on need: it does not need to be set as the goal of education. Instead, we can develop tools that can be used to engage all people – regardless of their literacy, English language skills, and/or access to (aspects of) material and non-material systems.

Moving forward...

The world around us is a mix of things – most of which we do not know or recognise. We make sense of the world that we encounter by using our sensory systems and developing and sharing interpretations of the stimulus we receive. Over time, as our ideas, thoughts, knowledge, beliefs, and goals change, our perception and engagement with the world changes too. And this engagement can impact and change the material-biological world through our actions or inactions.

At present, especially in the exploited communities, our sense making abilities have been crippled by colonial policies and practices. Fixing this is not an easy task. However, it is a feasible one because things that are socio-semiotic are, by definition, dynamic, and always fluid – thus, they can change to harmonise our societies and eco-systems.

In concluding this chapter, we will share a poem called, Symbols: A Translingual Poem (Figure 2.2). Note that the Urdu, Hindi, and Roman scripts represent the same sounds/boli in contrast to English that uses only one. The different and conflicting scripts – which are all symbols – used by Urdu/Hindi speakers is an outcome of British socio-semiotic violence. The British encouraged the use of two writing systems for the same boli (Urdu-Hindi, in their everyday registers, are mutually intelligible even today). And, by doing this, they created two languages out of one and cultivated the Hindu–Muslim divide that has turned a once-upon-a-prosperous-land into a nightmare. This is one reason Sunny Boy now refuses to name his language and instead simply calls his speech, 'boli'.

Making sense of the world 29

Figure 2.2 Symbols: A Translingual Poem by Sunny Boy. An audio-video version of the poem is available here: https://youtu.be/JiRyTYm2h8k

3 Moving forward with practice

> Come Nomad, you have seen enough,
> Unharnessed greed runs over the world
> Like a polluted river: spreading as he flows.
>
> Come Nomad, you have heard enough,
> Unashamed voices sing songs of lies
> Full of rhymes that silence sounds of pain.
>
> Come Nomad, you have learnt enough,
> Now walk towards a place of possibility
> Where we contribute to create harmony.
>
> Prof Nomad

Having recognised some of the colonial mischief hidden in academia and education that contribute to the exploitative and hegemonic policies and practices that many lives (human and non-human) experience today, we need to create and share alternative frameworks and approaches to move forward with practice.

Subaltern practice is work that empowers local and geographically relevant epistemologies (i.e., local ways of being, doing, and saying) by encouraging and supporting local economies, practices, projects, and resources. This work can be done by anyone and in any language/dialect. That's because subaltern linguistics is practice, not theory. One way of enabling subaltern practice is to adopt the CREDIBLE approach. This approach draws on the distinction between the material-biological and socio-semiotic worlds as well as engaging multiple/all sensory systems.

What is the CREDIBLE approach?

The CREDIBLE approach (see Figure 3.1) guides people to start their work with identification of an issue or problem that they want to address by designing and producing contextually relevant material and resources. As such, it responds to and is driven by practical needs

DOI: 10.4324/9781003495086-4

> Contextually relevant {think locally}
> Responds to practical needs {not driven by theory}
> Engages stakeholders {not restricted to data collection }
> Draws on an understanding of local knowledge and practices {pays attention to local beliefs, practices, and expression}
> Informed by diverse approaches and experiences {not just western}
> Benefits local communities {without benefit, there is little credibility in a project}
> Leads the field/discipline {projects that address real-world local issues lead the field by providing models for others}
> Ethical {responsible and respectful; not just having consent forms signed}

Figure 3.1 The CREDIBLE approach

rather than theoretical questions. To do this work, the project team collaborates with and includes other stakeholders, whoever these might be. By doing so, CREDIBLE projects avoid exploiting people for data that serves only academics and their interests. To engage with stakeholders, it is essential that we are sensitive to local ways of being and doing. At the same time, to develop the project, we also need to look at examples of similar or relevant work in other parts of the world. By developing material and resources to address a community need, we can benefit the community. And, when this work is done ethically, it becomes a model for others and moves the field forward.

We chose the acronym CREDIBLE to develop our work for a few reasons. One key reason was to contrast credibility with the more commonly used measures of 'reliability' and 'validity' in research. Drawing on a subaltern perspective, we observe that issues of reliability and validity are only relevant if a project is CREDIBLE. If a project brings no real benefits, then – even if it is reliable and valid – it is not CREDIBLE and hence not necessarily worth our time, attention, or resources.

To create CREDIBLE projects, we need to observe and learn from case studies by engaging in Positive Discourse Analysis (PDA). We will discuss how to plan and carry out CREDIBLE projects and PDA in detail in Part III of this book. In this chapter we will briefly introduce some key concepts that will be extended in later parts of the book.

Appropriate case studies for CREDIBLE projects and PDA use understandings of material-biological and socio-semiotic systems to influence action and change in a community. If there is evidence of change and influence, then we have a case study for PDA. For example, the Australian anti-tobacco campaign has been successful because the rates of smoking in Australia have reduced, and teenage uptake of smoking has decreased. Thus, we can carry out a PDA of the Australian anti-tobacco campaign to learn how it achieved its goals.

And, in turn, we can use our learning from this and other case studies to design material for issues that are relevant to our context.

Positive Discourse Analysis can be both broad and narrow. In this book, we will mostly focus on broad PDA [a narrow PDA requires different tools of analysis, as will be briefly discussed in Chapter 4]. A broad PDA has two goals: 1) to review examples and case studies of successful projects by analysing how the project achieved its goals; and 2) to design and implement projects that draw on local material-biological and socio-semiotic resources to benefit one's own community and environment.

To achieve these goals, we draw on broad PDA to analyse multiple case studies and then plan and execute a project that responds to a local issue by respecting the local material-biological, and socio-semiotic resources. In searching for projects to use as case studies, it is useful to collect examples from diverse sources and regions, as each place and people have different ways of being, thinking, and doing. We can learn from and invest in diversity.

PDA is a complementary approach to the popular Critical Discourse Analysis (CDA). However, in contrast to CDA, which often explores how power impacts communities by looking for patterns and causes of oppression in discourse, PDA is focused on looking at good practices and solutions to real-world problems. PDA is not focused on examining discourses for the sake of examining discourses; PDA is about doing. PDA is not about identifying power structures that disable us; rather, it is about creating alternatives and possibilities for people to improve themselves on their own terms and by doing things that they want to do. To do PDA, we can look at successful projects from around the world – not just the west (or in English) – and consider questions such as: how are these projects/materials designed? what sensory systems are drawn upon (explicitly and metaphorically)? what socio-semiotics are assumed and/or projected?

Below, we share four examples of CREDIBLE projects that were developed by others. Part II of the book provides many more examples of projects carried out by our students and colleagues for a range of purposes. And additional examples are shared in Part III and Part IV of this book.

Example 1: Australian anti-tobacco campaign

The Australian anti-tobacco campaign is an example of a successful project because it has resulted in a decrease in the use and uptake of tobacco/smoking. This project was multi-pronged and used advertisements, taxes, laws, and education to influence a change in the community. The advertisement material that it developed related to all five material senses and made one see, hear, smell, touch, and taste the negative impacts of tobacco.

Moving forward with practice   33

The campaign impacted vision and smell by enforcing laws and policies that prohibit smoking in public places, parks, school zones, restaurants, public transport, etc. This prohibition implies that smoking and smokers cannot be seen, heard, or smelt in many public places. An absence, or at least a reduction, of smoking and smokers in public spaces implies that children grow up with less exposure to smoking. This reduces the likelihood that they will grow up smoking.

The campaign included television, radio, and internet advertisements which shared sounds of people coughing or gasping for air. These sounds and associated visuals created a negative association of smoking with health and well-being. The material also implied that smoke smells bad and effects our ability to smell other things; that it leads to diseases with skin deformities and inflation – connecting to our sense of touch; and, that one can't taste food and other things well if one continues to smoke.

In addition, the campaign provided alternative discourses that projected positive images of how one's life can improve if one gives up smoking. It provided educational resources and materials. It projected the savings one can make along with the other benefits of quitting smoking. And, in doing all this, new jobs and sub-specialisations were created. For example, people were trained and employed to provide support to individuals who want to quit smoking.

A broad PDA of the Australian tobacco campaign demonstrates how an effective campaign relates to all our material senses, using multiple modes, along with advocating for and reaffirming particular socio-semiotics. For example, we can note how the advert (Figure 3.2) relates to all our sensory systems, even though it is only an image.

Table 3.1 provides a broad PDA of the advert to demonstrate how it relates to the five senses:

Here we see that even though the advert is an image, it can still metaphorically relate to all our sensory systems. In our observation,

Figure 3.2 An example of an anti-tobacco advert produced by the Australian government

Table 3.1 Broad PDA of the advert presented in Figure 3.2

	Description	What meanings are being projected?
Sight	Image of pregnant woman	The image of the pregnant woman takes up a large proportion of the poster meaning our attention is drawn to her. Once we look at her, we can see she is smiling and looking down at her belly, which suggests to the viewer that she is happy, which creates an overall positive feeling towards the poster.
	Language	The language works in conjunction with the image by telling pregnant women how to be healthy during pregnancy. It provides tips for how to manage cravings and explains the benefits of not smoking during pregnancy. The language also tells pregnant women of the quitting resources available such as Quitline to further encourage them to quit smoking.
	Light and pale colours	Looking at the poster as a whole, the light and pale colours used create a light, positive and calming effect which is needed during pregnancy.
Sound	Quitline number	The Quitline number is provided for pregnant women who need support to quit smoking. This is important as it caters for women who do not have high literacy to read all the language on the poster or read information on the website.
Smell	The letter Q	The letter Q in Quit and Quitline are in the shape of a cigarette with a stop sign which can project the bad smell of cigarettes.
Touch	Pregnant woman holding belly	The pregnant woman on the poster is holding her belly which can give pregnant women a sense of how it will feel when they actually hold their own baby. This again encourages pregnant women to quit smoking, so they get the chance to hold their baby.
Taste	The letter Q	The letter Q in Quit and Quitline are in the shape of a cigarette with a stop sign which can project the bad taste of cigarettes.

we note that effective marketing and public education messaging tends to be more effective if it relates to multiple sensory systems.

Let us now review how this was a CREDIBLE project:

Contextually relevant: the material was developed by the Australian government for the Australian public as part of a public education campaign against smoking.

Responds to practical needs: smoking can contribute to various health problems, and it is necessary to create campaigns to reduce the rates of smoking.

Moving forward with practice   35

Engages stakeholders: the material was developed in coordination between various government and non-governmental organisations and shared with the public via media outlets.

Draws on an understanding of local knowledge and practices: the strategies and material developed as part of this campaign were designed with an understanding of local practices and socio-semiotics.

Informed by diverse approaches and experiences: the designers of the campaign drew on multiple disciplines and frameworks to develop the campaign.

Benefits local communities: a reduction in the rate of smoking helps improve the health of the people in the community.

Leads and contributes to the field: the Australian anti-tobacco campaign has been producing the results intended for a few decades now and is an example for others to learn from.

Ethical: the goals of the project were to improve individual and community health.

Example 2: Cherokee syllabary

Sequoyah was a Cherokee person (Cherokee is an Indigenous group in North America) who realised that the occupiers who captured their lands used writing to create and maintain power (Figure 3.3). Cherokee, at that point did not have a writing system. Sequoyah set out – with no training in linguistics – to develop a writing system for his boli. He first experimented with a phonetic system but realised that it did not suit his purposes. He therefore invented a set of characters that were syllabic, not phonetic. Once he had completed his script and published it, the Cherokee script spread quickly through his community. Sequoyah's

a	e	i	o	u	v [ə]
D a	R e	T i	Ꮼ o	Ꮓ u	i v
Ꮝ ga Ꮣ ka	Ꮈ ge	Ᏹ gi	A go	J gu	E gv
Ꮈ ha	Ꮉ he	Ꮎ hi	Ꮈ ho	Γ hu	Ꮕ hv
W la	Ꮈ le	P li	G lo	M lu	Ꭹ lv
Ꮿ ma	Cl me	H mi	Ꮹ mo	Y mu	
Θ na Ꮑ hna G nah	Ꮒ ne	Ꮒ ni	Z no	Ꮕ nu	Ꮕ nv
Ꮨ qua	Ꮕ que	Ꮖ qui	Ꮖ quo	Ꮖ quu	Ꮖ quv
Ꮝ s Ꮜ sa	Ꮞ se	Ꮟ si	Ꮠ so	Ꮡ su	R sv
Ꮤ da W ta	Ꮥ de Ꮦ te	Ꮧ di Ꮨ ti	V do	S du	Ꮩ dv
Ꮪ dla Ꮫ tla	L tle	C tli	Ꮭ tlo	Ꮮ tlu	P tlv
G tsa	V tse	Ir tsi	K tso	Ꮰ tsu	C tsv
G wa	Ꮼ we	Θ wi	Ꮽ wo	Ꮾ wu	6 wv
Ꮿ ya	Ᏸ ye	Ꮵ yi	Ꮶ yo	G yu	B yv

Figure 3.3 Cherokee syllabary (photo from Wikimedia Commons)

script, which is a socio-semiotic resource, is still used today and is one reason why the Cherokee people and language were able to survive the onslaughts of occupation, colonisation, and genocide.

Sequoyah can be considered a champion of subaltern linguistics and CREDIBLE projects. He saw a need in his community and addressed it by creating a new writing system – a writing system that is arguably much better than the phonetic scripts used and promoted by colonial linguistics.

The Cherokee syllabary project is a CREDIBLE one because:

> **C**ontextually relevant: Cherokee language did not have a writing system and, in the onslaught of occupation, one was needed to maintain the language and Indigenous knowledge.
>
> **R**esponds to practical needs: Sequoyah observed the need for developing a writing system to be able to resist occupation and colonisation, and to maintain their culture and heritage.
>
> **E**ngages stakeholders: Sequoyah was a member of the Cherokee community and worked with other members of his community.
>
> **D**raws on an understanding of local knowledge and practices: Sequoyah developed a script that worked best for the local language.
>
> **I**nformed by diverse approaches and experiences: Sequoyah learnt about the various ways in which writing systems can operate and chose to develop a syllabic system.
>
> **B**enefits local communities: the development and publishing of the script allowed for members of his community to develop literacy practices that helped them maintain their culture and practices.
>
> **L**eads and contributes to the field: the Cherokee syllabary continues to be a model script for other Indigenous languages.
>
> **E**thical: Sequoyah, an Indigenous person, created a resource for his own community that helped the community maintain its language and other socio-semiotic practices.

Example 3: Smiling Mind meditation app

The Aboriginal peoples of Australia are among the oldest living populations in the world, and have the oldest living culture, having occupied the mainland of Australia for at least 65,000 years. Aboriginal people have always had a profound connection to the land. It is intrinsically linked to their language, culture, laws, and health. However, with the invasion of the British in 1788, this connection to the land was abruptly disrupted with the forced removal of Aboriginal people from their homes and land. This dispossession has been directly linked to poor physical and mental health outcomes in Aboriginal peoples in Australia.

Moving forward with practice   37

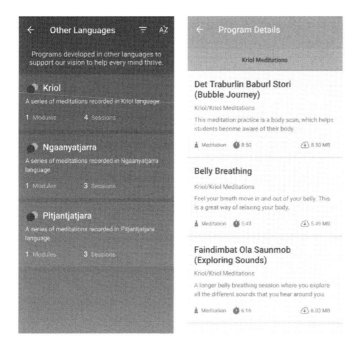

Figure 3.4 & 3.5 Meditation programs and activities in Kriol, Ngaanyatjarra and Pitjantjatjara - screen shots taken by Aurelie

Today, the incidence of mental illness among the Indigenous peoples of Australia is significantly higher than non-Indigenous Australians. To improve the mental health and well-being of Indigenous communities, women from Central Australia's Ngaanyatjarra Pitjantjatjara Yankunytjatjara Women's Council (NPYWC), teamed up with the producers of the Smiling Mind app, a non-for-profit mindfulness meditation app, to record a series of meditations in three Australian Indigenous languages: Kriol, Ngaanyatjarra and Pitjantjiatjara. Figure 3.4 and Figure 3.5 illustrates a screenshot of the program developed in the three Indigenous languages, and some of the meditation activities in Kriol.

The Smiling Mind app was initially developed in Ngaanyatjarra and Pitjantjiatjara, and then working with school staff and the community in Jilkminggan in the Northern Territory, the meditations were also translated into Kriol, as shown in Figure 3.4. This shows how the project expanded to also include another language and a new set of users: children. It shows how when we create a project that addresses practical needs, the project has the potential to expand and be used in new contexts.

Mindfulness is about being fully present in the moment and allowing your thoughts to float by without attaching any opinions, judgements, or preferences to them. Mindfulness can be practiced in our everyday lives while engaging in our daily activities or it can be practiced through meditation.

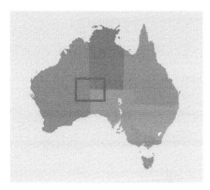

Figure 3.6 Map of cross-border region of Northern Territory, South Australia, and Western Australia

The Indigenous mindfulness series adopted the latter approach to mindfulness training. It contains evidence-based programs such as breathing exercises, meditation, and singing for 28 Indigenous communities in the cross-border region of Northern Territory, South Australia and Western Australia, highlighted in the red square in Figure 3.6.

The app combines knowledge from ngangkari (traditional healers) and western psychologists and health professionals to provide a program in the languages of the Indigenous communities that is also culturally appropriate for the mental wellbeing of the Indigenous communities. The app is a part of the Council's Uti Kulintjaku project, translated to "to think and understand clearly" which began in 2012 to improve education around mental health and wellbeing. Having been downloaded by thousands of people, the world's first ever Indigenous language mindfulness program was also used in schools in remote South Australia.

The Smiling Mind app of the Uti Kulintjaku project is an example of how community members can undertake a project that addresses local needs, benefits the local community, and empowers its people. Furthermore, it demonstrates how outside stakeholders and local stakeholders can collaborate and draw on their diverse expertise to create a program that can have a beneficial impact on people's mental wellbeing.

The Smiling Mind app project is a CREDIBLE project because:

> **C**ontextually relevant: the Smiling Mind app is contextually relevant as it was specifically designed to address mental health issues in the 28 Indigenous communities of Central Australia.
>
> **R**esponds to practical needs: the Smiling Mind app was designed to combat mental health issues in these 28 Indigenous communities by using mindfulness and breathing exercises, among other techniques, and therefore responds to the communities' practical needs.
>
> **E**ngages stakeholders: one of the wonderful aspects of the mindfulness app is the various stakeholders involved in creating the app.

> In creating the app, the women of the NPYWC involved ngangkari (traditional healers) with interpreters and western mental health professionals. Working with the ngangkari meant that they were able to understand how mindfulness could be understood in their context in a culturally appropriate way.
>
> **D**raws on an understanding of local knowledge and practices: the creators of the Smiling Mind app drew on knowledge from traditional healers and Indigenous peoples to create a culturally appropriate app.
>
> **I**nformed by diverse approaches and experiences: the developers of the app not only utilised traditional knowledge and practices but also drew from western psychologists and health professionals to develop the app.
>
> **B**enefits local communities: this is also clearly evident in the Smiling Mind app project which was specifically designed to benefit the local Indigenous communities of Central Australia by combatting mental health issues.
>
> **L**eads and contributes to the field: the Smiling Mind app was initially developed in Ngaanyatjarra and Pitjantjiatjara, then working with school staff and the community in Jilkminggan in the Northern Territory, the meditations were also translated into Kriol. This shows how the project expanded to also include another language and a new set of users: children. It shows how when we create a project that addresses practical needs, the project has the potential to expand and be used in new contexts.
>
> **E**thical: the Smiling Mind app of the Uti Kulintjaku project is an excellent example of how community members can undertake a project that addresses local needs, benefits the local community, and empowers its people. Furthermore, it demonstrates how outside stakeholders and local stakeholders can collaborate and draw on their diverse expertise to create a program that can have a beneficial impact on people's mental wellbeing.

Example 4: "Free Throw Plastic Bottles"

Another example of an independent CREDIBLE project developed by people in a community is the design and installation of a disposal unit for plastic bottles in Pasacao, Camarines Sur, in the Philippines. Using an understanding of how Filipinos love basketball, John Robrigado, a local youth councillor, designed and installed a "Free Throw Plastic Bottles" area to encourage people to discard plastic bottles in a safe manner. This project uses language, understanding of people, and some engineering to design a garbage collector for plastic bottles. As such, it is an example of subaltern practice: an application of socio-semiotics for the betterment of people and the environment (Figure 3.7).

Figure 3.7 "Free Throw Plastic Bottles", Pasacao, Camarines Sur, Philippines. Image sourced from social media

In teaching language/linguistics, we should share such examples and encourage others to develop projects for and with the community. Language/linguistics is not really about grammar rules and pronunciation; it is about the use of language to benefit our communities.

We can analyse this project to see how it is CREDIBLE:

Contextually relevant: the "Free Throw Plastic Bottles" project was developed for and by community members to help reduce trash in the community.

Responds to practical needs: plastic bottles contribute to environmental problems and this project helped to reduce such waste in the community.

Engages stakeholders: the project was developed by locals in collaboration with the local government. The design of the trash receptacle directly engages with the community members by getting them to throw their bottles properly.

Draws on an understanding of local knowledge and practices: John Robrigado noted how Filipinos love basketball and designed the trash receptacle in the image of a basketball court.

Informed by diverse approaches and experiences: the project drew on understandings of how plastic trash harms the environment and a study of ways in which it can be reduced.

Benefits local communities: a reduction in pollution benefits both the environment and people.

Leads and contributes to the field: the design of the trash receptacle is unique and can be adapted in other places.

Ethical: the goals of the project were to reduce environmental degradation.

While the "Free Throw Plast Bottles" project is a good example of how socio-semiotics are used to create a resource, the design can be enhanced in many ways. For example, there can be an additional hole in a lower part of the "court" so that people who are unable to throw can still discard their plastic waste in an appropriate manner. In addition, there could be signage that educates people about the harms of plastic and pollution. This signage can be images with supporting text in local languages and can be designed by local communities. Making, placing, and maintaining such projects can create jobs for people in local communities; jobs that give economic incentives to people to maintain their languages and to use their languages to empower themselves. In addition to enabling an economy in the local languages, it will also create a greater involvement of the community in developing its own resources and material.

This project can also be expanded and other measures brought into place. The purpose of these measures could be to educate the communities in ways that help them. The current school curriculum in many parts of the world has little to teach children about the places where they live and grow up; and more to do with faraway places and abstract ideas that are often not relevant to one's own context. One reason for this is an over-emphasis on books and reading, and less on doing. And many of the corporate-published textbooks today, which are considered the "best" in the developing world, are written to train children to work for corporations and endorse the values of the corporate/colonial world.

Instead, educational curricula can be conceived as ways of educating our students about doing things. By learning how to engage with communities, they can learn ways to create and do things that respect and are in sync with local ways of being. Such a curriculum would need to be designed with a vision of how the community sees itself to be.

Education is successful when our students develop projects that aid in community empowerment. Such projects raise students' self-esteem and self-respect, two key goals of education. In current schooling in many parts of the world today, tests and assessments negatively impact students' self-esteem and self-respect; and they graduate with a belief that the west has the answers and that living in the west is a desired goal. Their low self-esteem – for themselves and their communities – leads them to imagine a "better life" elsewhere. If we want to keep our people home and enable them to become participatory citizens, we have to develop economies in and through our own languages and boost the self-esteem and self-respect of our peoples.

Part II

What are CREDIBLE projects?

In this part of the book, we show what CREDIBLE projects can look like when addressing different issues in communities. These projects were mostly carried out by Applied Linguistics postgraduate students at the University of Sydney and demonstrate that CREDIBLE can be applied in various fields. These projects can also serve as models for replication in different settings and communities.

Chapter 4 starts off Part II with projects for education, including developing materials to support online learning, and the *How to Write* resources that scaffold students into writing for specialised purposes. Next, Chapter 5 looks at projects for the environment such as educating residents in Foshan, China on sorting garbage; encouraging consumers in Sydney to choose reusable coffee cups; and teaching students in Santiago, Chile, about recycling.

Then, Chapter 6 explores projects for health and wellbeing including combating misinformation on Overseas Student Health Cover in Sydney, teaching primary school children in Xiamen, China on the dangers of sweetened beverages, and the Trash Project which draws links between trash and health and environmental issues. Finally, Chapter 7 describes projects for economic development, specifically showcasing Language Travels in Malacca, Malaysia that addressed the language endangerment of Kristang for the Malaccan Portuguese community and shares plans about future Language Travels projects for other communities.

4 CREDIBLE projects for education

Now that we have seen what CREDIBLE projects can look like, it is time to be inspired further by examples where CREDIBLE has been applied in different fields. In the next few chapters, we will explore multiple projects in different communities addressing a wide array of issues.

These are some of the standout projects selected from the final projects of postgraduate students enrolled in the unit of study, LNGS7002 Language Society and Power, LNGS 7102 Educational Linguistics, and LNGS 7501 Professional Practice at the University of Sydney, Australia. Most of these projects were carried out between the years of 2019 and 2022.

The CREDIBLE approach was introduced to postgraduate students enrolled in LNGS7002. They were then tasked with carrying out a CREDIBLE project in their own community as a final assignment. A key step in practicing CREDIBLE is to first identify an issue that is embedded within a community. Some students worked in groups while others did their projects individually. Whether developed by a group or individual, the projects showcased in these chapters are real world examples that demonstrate how CREDIBLE is appliable and achievable, regardless of which fields the issues lie in. The education sector is perhaps where we see more obviously the role of appliable linguistics. In this chapter, we look at two examples of CREDIBLE projects in education.

The first is where teachers need support when it comes to integrating the use of technology in their classrooms. In this project, we see how Regan Gauci chose to address the issue of the sudden migration from face-to-face to online learning. The use of Positive Discourse Analysis (PDA) was useful in designing her materials and the framework directed Regan towards a strong focus on goal setting and achievement. The CREDIBLE approach led to her thoughtful consideration of the significance of the project to the community and the strong connection between reviewing literature and materials and designing and conducting the project.

The second example is focused on addressing the issue of students in need of learning resources that work effectively to bridge the gap between knowledge and practice. We will look at two workbooks

DOI: 10.4324/9781003495086-6

developed by students in LNGS 7102, led by Sunny Boy. *How to Write: Receiving and Admission Nursing Notes* was authored by James Duncan, Jian Jiao, Yao Li, Yunqi Ma, Hye Ryun Park, Zichen Xu, and Weiwei Zheng. And *How to Write: A Literature Review for Project Development* was authored by Mona Aqeel, Lungguh Ariang Bangga, Zheng Cai, Jiani Chen, Lin Chen, Renee Constantin, Magno Da Silva, Haiyi Feng, Lee Cheng Koay, Xiaoting Liang, Puxin Mo, Yuet Fu Ng, Hong Pan, Suhuan Pei, Kaiying Shen, Xiao Su, Xinshuang Wang, Jiawen Wu, Kaihua Wu, Zhizhou Wu, Jingyu Yang, Lei Yang, Huiyu Zhang, and Jiaqi Zhang. The development of these learning resources relied on PDA to model language features and build students confidence through step-by-step reasoning and practice.

Example 1: Supporting online teaching

In recent years – and especially during the COVID period – we have seen a shift from traditional classroom-style teaching to more hybrid and online environments where the use of technology is incorporated.

Teachers in New South Wales need to adhere to the industry's professional standards to ensure students are receiving quality teaching. In NSW, the Australian Professional Standards for Teachers (APST) (2011) was validated by the Australian Institute for Teaching and School Leadership (AITSL) (Figure 4.1). AITSL is an organisation founded by the Australian Government to promote and support excellence in teaching and school leadership.

APST is used by teachers to develop their teaching expertise. With the growing use of technology in the classrooms, we can see that it impacts the areas 2, 3, and 4 of Professional Knowledge and Professional Practice in APST[1]. This can present a challenge to teachers who would need to learn not only how to operate the technology, but also how to teach with it, direct students to use it, and maintain a safe environment.

When COVID-19 first hit the shores of New South Wales, everything began to go into lockdown and classrooms moved into the digital world, depending more than ever on technology for teaching. Regan Gauci worked at the English learning centre in Cabramatta as a teacher of English as an Additional Language or Dialect (EAL/D) and found herself and her co-workers facing a difficult challenge: migrate face-to-face teaching to online teaching in two days.

Regan used the CREDIBLE approach to enhance teaching practices at Cabramatta Intensive English Centre and develop learning materials for her program. In particular, she drew on PDA to create effective lesson plans that ensured that the quality of teaching was maintained, while providing adequate guidance and confidence to the teachers carrying it out.

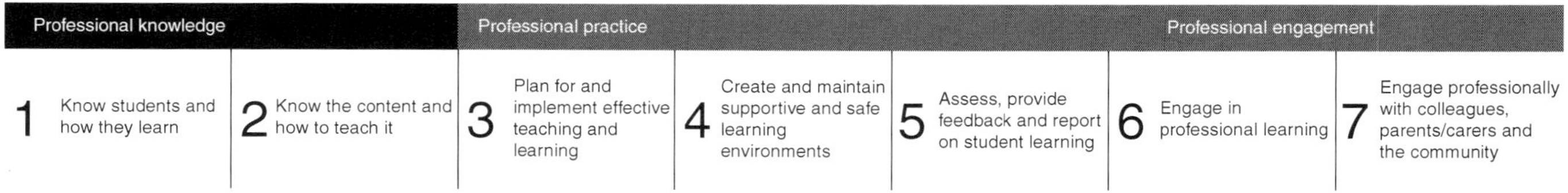

CREDIBLE projects for education 47

Professional knowledge		Professional practice			Professional engagement	
1 Know students and how they learn	2 Know the content and how to teach it	3 Plan for and implement effective teaching and learning	4 Create and maintain supportive and safe learning environments	5 Assess, provide feedback and report on student learning	6 Engage in professional learning	7 Engage professionally with colleagues, parents/carers and the community

Figure 4.1 The seven standards relate to three professional domains. Source: Australian Institute for Teaching and School Leadership[1]

Through her research and observations, she found that there were many factors that could impact a teacher's ability to adapt to online lesson delivery. Some of these include unfamiliarity with pedagogical approaches to online learning, lack of and poor access to professional learning opportunities related to technology in educational contexts, and lack of EAL/D training.

Regan designed her project to achieve two key goals: (1) To assist teachers in designing effective online learning materials for EAL/D learners; (2) To provide EAL/D students with quality online learning in lieu of face to face classroom learning.

Based on those goals, her target community were the teachers at Cabramatta Intensive English Centre (IEC) and by default the students who received the lessons. The materials included a model lesson plan that focused on the joint-construction phase of the teaching and learning cycle, lesson materials related to the lesson plan, and a sample of student work. Regan had to also align her materials with the content and outcomes of the Intensive English Program Curriculum Framework, as it is the main syllabus document that both teachers and students within the target community of this project were familiar with.

Just like all her peers in the unit of study, Regan started with a literature and material review. She researched the specific issues that teachers were having in regard to online learning and the pedagogical approaches to online teaching and learning within the context of EAL/D students. Using what she found in her review, she began to design her materials for the project. A sample lesson plan is shared in Figure 4.2.

It was apparent in her final products that Regan constantly kept in mind that while the materials needed to be easily accessible and highly applicable, they should not come across as patronising to experienced EAL/D trained teachers. Additionally, a feature that Regan was able to craft within her materials was the inclusion of the eight Aboriginal Ways of Learning (Eight Ways) pedagogy to ensure that her project was informed by diverse approaches and expressions.

Eight Ways is a pedagogical framework for teachers to use Aboriginal learning techniques and to include Aboriginal perspectives in their classroom learning. The Eight Ways are:

- Story sharing (approaching learning through narrative);
- Learning maps (explicit visualisation processes);
- Non-verbal (applying intra-personal and kinaesthetic skills to thinking and learning);
- Symbols and images (using images and metaphors to understand concepts and content);
- Land links (place-based learning, linking content to local land and place);

CREDIBLE projects for education   49

Taste it for culture

Class:	2S		Date:	26th of May, 28th of May and 1st of June 2020
No. of students:	12		Length:	3 × 60 minute face to face lessons
Subject	Topic Focus	Text types	Unit description	Learning intention	Mode of delivery
EAL/D	Cultural significance of food	Procedure Description	To understand the significance of food to cultural heritage and practices, students jointly and independently deconstruct and reconstruct a procedure (recipe) by cooking a culturally significant recipe. The teacher first models their own recipe, cooking with the students. The class then jointly constructs a procedure (recipe). Finally, students cook something significant to them with a family member, and independently write this into a recipe. Students later reflect on the significance of this through composing a description.	Students will be able to: - Understand the cultural significance of food and cooking - Understand the structure and language features of the text type - Independently write a procedure (recipe)	• Online – through google classroom and zoom

IEPCF Outcomes	K-10 English stage 4 outcomes	8 Aboriginal ways of learning
Level 2 7 – Reads and/or views and comprehends an informative text: procedure and description 12 – Composes and informative text: procedure and description	EN4-3B – uses and describes language forms, features and structures of texts appropriate to a range of purposes, audiences and contexts EN4-8D – identifies, considers and appreciates cultural expression in texts EN4-9E – uses, reflects on and assesses their individual and collaborative skills for learning	Story sharing: Approaching learning through narrative [Personal narratives (stories) are central] Learning maps: Explicitly mapping/visualising processes [images or visuals are used to map out processes for learners to follow] Non-verbal: Applying intra-personal and kinaesthetic skills to thinking and learning [Kinaesthetic, hands-on, non-verbal learning is characteristic] Deconstruct/Reconstruct: Modelling and scaffolding, working from wholes to parts [Begin with the whole structure, rather than a series of sequenced steps. Holistic, global, scaffolded and independent learning orientations of students] Community links: Centring local viewpoints, applying learning for community benefit [Connections to real-life purposes, contexts and communities and teams]

Students learn about	Students learn to	Target language features	
• The cultural significance of food and cooking • The structure of procedures (specifically recipes) • The language features of recipes	• Apply prior knowledge and learning to a set task • Construct a procedure (recipe), following the correct text structure and including the appropriate language features	Procedural text technical vocabulary, imperative verbs, infinitives, connectives and passive voice	Description technical vocabulary, noun groups, verbs ('to be' and 'to have'), simple present tense, conjunctions and adverbial phrases

Pre-lesson activities
- 'Traditional maltese food' online activity (reading comprehension) - Ħobż biż-zjt recipe list

Figure 4.2 Sample lesson plan created by Regan

Figure 4.3 Photograph of Ħobż biż-żejt, a popular Maltese snack

- Non-linear (producing innovations and understanding by thinking laterally or combining systems);
- Deconstruct/reconstruct (modelling and scaffolding, working from wholes to parts – watch then do); and
- Community links (centring local viewpoints, applying learning for community benefit).

In Figure 4.2, we see Regan incorporating the Eight Ways in her lesson plan. She taught her students English using a traditional Maltese recipe from her heritage to draw their interest and build value around their own culture. Figures 4.3 and 4.4 share more examples from Regan's project.

Regan's materials were well-received by students and teachers. She saw engaged students in the Zoom classes that she ran during the period of conducting her project. Her collaborators at Cabramatta IEC remained supportive of her work throughout as well. This example shows how people can develop CREDIBLE projects for their own contexts and needs by drawing on the strategies and methods shared in Part III of this book.

Example 2: The "How to Write…" workbooks

The "How to Write" resources were developed by students in the LNGS 7102 Educational Linguistics unit of study. We will look at the two "How to Write…" workbooks – *How to Write: Receiving and Admission Nursing Notes* and *How to Write: A Literature Review for Project Development* – that have been created so far. The development of both books took a CREDIBLE approach in that the issue was embedded within a community and the projects were carried out by students and relevant collaborators to help address the issues.

Ħobż biż-żejt

Ingredients

1 slice of crusty sourdough bread
1 tablespoon of extra virgin olive oil
2 tablespoon of tomato paste
Salt and pepper to taste
1 small can of tuna
1 small tin of anchovies
1/4 sliced onion
1 teaspoon of capers

Equipment

A chopping board
1 butter knife
1 tablespoon
1 teaspoon

Serving size

Serves 1

Method

1. Take one slice of crusty bread and place it on a chopping board

2. Spread one teaspoon of olive oil all over the bread

3. Use a knife to spread some tomato paste all over the bread

4. Spoon some tuna onto the bread

5. Place some anchovies on top of the tuna

6. Put some sliced onion on top of the anchovies

7. Sprinkle some capers on top of the onion

8. Add a small amount of salt and pepper

Enjoy!

Figure 4.4 The Ħobż biż-żejt recipe was one of Regan's topics of focus

For both workbooks, the use of PDA was critical. The developers drew on Systemic Functional Linguistics (SFL) and the Teaching Learning Cycle (TLC) to create the materials. While the other examples in this book have drawn on a broad PDA, the authors of both workbooks drew on narrow PDA, which requires a different set of tools and resources. In developing the workbooks, the students applied register analysis based SFL to carry out a narrow PDA. Register analysis is an analytical framework that is able to provide a system of linguistic choices that support the function of the text. This framework was chosen because it looks at language through its function within a particular context, rather than a set of rigid rules of grammar.

Since the workbooks also applied TLC, the authors used register analysis to identify linguistic features within ideal sample text. These features were then explicitly highlighted, shown and explained to the reader. This stage of teaching is called Deconstruction in TLC and exemplified in Figures 4.5 and 4.6.

Then, the users of the workbooks were led into a guided activity that lets them write specific parts of the text. Instructions and guiding points were clearly laid out for the users so that they would be supported in their writing. This stage of TLC is known as Joint Construction and it gives the reader an opportunity to apply what they have learnt in a scaffolded setting. Examples of the Joint Construction activities from the two workbooks are shared in Figures 4.7 and 4.8.

The last section of the resource focused on the users writing independently, or Independent Construction in TLC (see Figures 4.9 and 4.10 for examples from the workbooks). If at any point a user was unable to complete the activity, they were encouraged to refer back to the earlier sections that included explicit explanations and/or the guided activity. Once they found their confidence in the matter, they could attempt the independent writing activities again. This cycle of

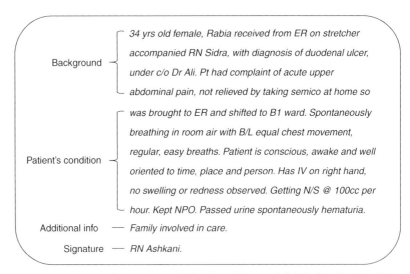

Figure 4.5 Excerpt from *How to Write: Receiving and Admission Nursing Notes* showing how a nursing admission note is written

CREDIBLE projects for education

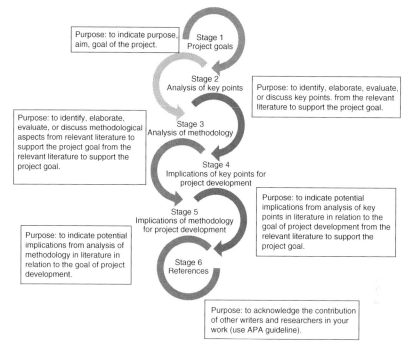

Figure 4.6 Excerpt from *How to Write: A Literature Review for Project Development* showing the stages of a literature review for project development based on its language features

teaching-learning based on TLC is a structured way of bridging the gap between knowing about something and actually doing it.

TLC can be applied in many different contexts. You will see how Part III of this book draws on TLC to scaffold you, our readers, into creating your own CREDIBLE project independently. In Chapter 8, we deconstruct a CREDIBLE project; in Chapter 9, we scaffold a jointly constructed project; and in Chapter 10, we encourage you to develop your own independent project.

The How to Write: Receiving and Admission Nursing Notes (www.academia.edu/35932456/How_to_Write_Receiving_and_Admission_Nursing_Notes) was born out of the need to support nurses and nursing students to write accurate and concise nursing notes. Drawing on the NurD (Nursing Documentation) Project, which aimed to support nursing students' English language and literacy needs at the Aga Khan University (AKU), Pakistan, this workbook was a result of collaboration between Sunny Boy, their students, professional nurses at AKU, and nursing educators at AKU. The target community were nursing students at AKU who need to draft nursing notes in English. The material, even though developed for a specific context, has been very widely shared and used – which can be gauged by the number of downloads of the document by people around the globe.

54 Subaltern Linguistics

Activity 13. Revising a note to admission/receiving note

Below is an example of an admission/receiving note written in a writing style different from typical admission/receiving notes. Read the notes carefully and revise them based on what we learned from this unit. You can follow the steps below:

1. Identify information for each stage/phase
2. Remove any unnecessary information
3. Write down the information you identified in order, using strategies that we learned in C2

> *A patient named Sarah Hiraj was received from the morning staff. She is 21 years old. She was received on bed 2A. Her doctor was Dr. Ahmed, and he suggested a semi-solid diet for her. She seems to be fine with the diet. She is complaining about too much cough with small and yellow sputum. It seems a bit thick as well. She had frequent loose motions two months ago, and is wondering if it's relevant to the current symptoms. She is conscious, awake and well oriented to time, place and person. The patient doesn't have any known food or any other allergy. Moreover, there was no weight loss history or any skin issues. Neither were there any hair problems. She experienced minor constipation for the past 3 days since last Friday, but did not take any medicine for it. No problem with urine._____RN Salim*

Figure 4.7 Excerpt from *How to Write: Receiving and Admission Nursing Notes* showing a guided activity

CREDIBLE projects for education

Activity 11: Complete the project goals

Fill in the blanks for the following project goals.

[This study]   [investigates]   [The focus of the research]
[the difficulties that young newly arrived refugees face]   [My paper]
[the key issues in working with men from immigrant and refugee communities in Australia]   [The current paper]   [answers]   [is to explore]

1. _____ seeks to address the importance of local government provide material needs to assist refugees adapting to a new country.
2. The current study _____ the impact of the refugee experience.
3. The aim of the project _____ one main question by undertaking interviews with volunteers.
4. The goal of the research is to examine_____.
5. _____ examines the attitudes of refugee who seeks mental health care.
6. _____ discovers the impact of involuntary migration on the family health in order to identify specific health care issues related to refugee families in transition living in Australia.
7. This research explores_____.

Figure 4.8 Excerpt from *How to Write: A Literature Review for Project Development* showing a guided activity

The How to Write: A Literature Review for Project Development (www.academia.edu/38944484/How_to_Write_A_Literature_Review_for_Project_Development) was developed to help students write a literature review specifically for project development. This relates to projects where students can learn from past interventions and research. While there are many learning resources on writing a literature review, most are in relation to identifying gaps for research purposes, not project development. Also, some of the learning materials do not provide enough scaffolding for students to achieve the ideal level of writing for a literature review. Hence this workbook met the needs of students who needed to develop projects within their field of study.

Finally, a third addition to the *How to Write* series is *How to Write: A CREDIBLE project report*. This resource is being developed as complementary material for this book to assist anyone who wants to document their CREDIBLE projects. (This material is now ready and you can download a free copy via the online resources for this book.)

56 Subaltern Linguistics

Activity 14. Writing an admission/receiving note

You are to write an admission/receiving note based on the admission/receiving interview that we looked at in Unit B. Since the interview contains information obtained from interaction, we provide some observed information for you to include in your admission/receiving note.

> **Observation**
> a) The patient is breathing spontaneously on room air.
> b) The patient is conscious, awake and well-oriented to time, place, and person.

Use the information to write a complete admission/receiving note. You can follow the steps below:

1. Match each segment to stage/phase
2. Identify necessary information
3. Write an admission/receiving note based on what we learned in this unit

Key answers for Segments 1 and 2, and the Signature stage are provided.

> **Interaction**
>
> **Segment 1**   *Background: patient information, reason for admission*
> a. Between Pt. Ayesha Jamil and the nurse Farah Veljee
> b. Pt has had stomach cramps, vomiting and diarrhea since Saturday morning.
> c. Pain brought Pt. to hospital.
>
> **Segment 2**   *Background: changes of patient's condition*
> a. Has had loose motions, vomiting and abdominal pain
> b. Ate barbecue last Friday night
> c. Had 14 to 15 episodes of loose motions
> d. Gradually decreased to 2–3
> e. No loose motion now
> f. No complaint related to stool
> g. Having some unknown medicine for loose motion
> h. Had hardly 2–3 episodes of stools, soft
> i. No other complaints related to passing the stool
> j. Vomited after drinking or eating
> k. Had medicine, stopped vomiting, feel nausea now

Figure 4.9 Excerpt from *How to Write: Receiving and Admission Nursing Notes* showing independent construction

CREDIBLE projects for education   57

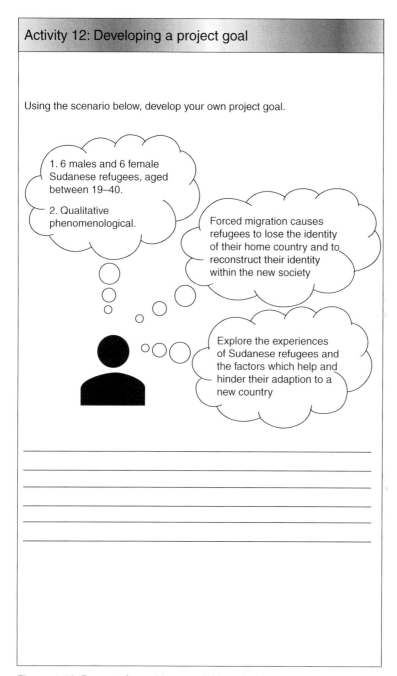

Figure 4.10 Excerpt from *How to Write: A Literature Review for Project Development* showing independent construction

As demonstrated in these two examples, CREDIBLE and PDA are key to developing these materials which address issues that tertiary students were facing.

In this chapter we have looked at how we can draw on the CREDIBLE approach to develop resources for educational contexts. In the next chapter we will look at CREDIBLE projects that focus on environmental issues.

Reference

Australian Professional Standards for Teachers. (2017). *Australian Institute for Teaching and School Leadership*. Retrieved from www.aitsl.edu.au/standards

5 CREDIBLE projects for the environment

Climate change and sustainability issues have become increasingly prominent and critical around the world. There is a sense of urgency to address issues relating to the environment because it directly impacts our future and the future of the generations to come. While governments around the world are addressing environmental issues through policies, it can take time before they are approved and properly implemented in communities. Hence, we see CREDIBLE projects which help address issues at the local level as one of the ways we can care for our environment effectively.

In this chapter we will consider three examples of CREDIBLE projects for the environment. The first project was led by Chu Yuan, Xinyi Zhang, and Yuelin Feng and dealt with helping a community create a system for garbage sorting where there was none in place. Having a collaborator with the authority needed to effect the change was crucial and by working together, they were able to tailor their materials to fit the needs of the community.

The second project by Li Yang, Alexis O'Connor, and Ying Yue Chen considered the impact of single-use coffee cups in a context where coffee is frequently consumed. The students faced several challenges in designing and implementing their material. Their project demonstrated the crucial role a collaborator has in helping navigate around potential issues in implementation.

The third project by Mariana Sáez Minchala and Chihiro Ohta, focused on educating school children about the purpose of recycling and gave them an opportunity to design recycling bins for their own school in a bin-designing contest.

Example 1: Educating on garbage sorting

Garbage sorting may seem an easy task but not everyone is aware of how to do it properly, especially if it has not been a habit cultivated from young (Figure 5.1). In recent years, local governments across China have begun to take garbage sorting seriously to reduce waste. Chu Yuan noted that more developed areas in the world have a more mature system of garbage sorting, but China's is relatively young. Even

DOI: 10.4324/9781003495086-7

Figure 5.1 Four pages from the children's colouring book

though cities like Shanghai first implemented regulations for garbage sorting in 2019, other cities, such as Foshan, have been slower on the uptake of such policies.

Chu Yuan, Xinyi Zhang, and Yuelin Feng found that their target community, a residential building complex in Li Hu Ming Xuan, Foshan, did not have facilities and posters to educate the residents about garbage sorting. As a result, the residents threw different types of garbage into the same bin. To tackle this issue, their project aimed to improve and raise awareness of the garbage sorting system in the community. The students reached out to the strata manager of the community to collaborate on the project.

The materials in this project were made to target two specific groups in the community – posters for adults and a colouring book for children. It was important that the materials were tailored to the target community and utilised the local languages of the community. The slogan on the posters aligned with the residents' first language, Cantonese, while also using Mandarin for other residents who do not speak Cantonese.

The colouring book was specifically designed for children in the residential complex who can influence a change in behaviour of their elders. The colouring book contained many task-based activities for the children to ignite their interest around the principles of garbage sorting. The language used in the book was simple with explicit instructions on how to complete the activity. Chinese Pinyin was added to the book to help children learn and understand the characters.

The character 靓 in Figure 5.2 is Cantonese and means "beauty". It was used to signify how appropriate garbage sorting can make things

CREDIBLE projects for the environment   61

Figure 5.2 Poster designs to educate the community on garbage sorting

cleaner and more beautiful. Each poster represented one type of garbage and the relevant bins they were meant to be thrown in. Colours were used to distinguish different kinds of waste according to Foshan city's policies: red was for hazardous garbage, green for kitchen waste, grey for other waste, and blue for recyclable garbage. The poster was displayed in elevators and on notice boards around the residential complex to inform the residents about the project and resources available for them.

The final part of the project focused on delivering the materials to the target community. With the help of their collaborator, the students were able to join a WeChat group for the residents in the community, and through that medium they were able to publish their materials and interact with the community further. Chapter 9 will elaborate further on this garbage sorting project and will also encourage you to jointly construct an environmental protection project within your own context.

Example 2: Choose to reuse

For this project the focus was on behavioural change specifically targeted at coffee drinkers. In this case, the target community was the students and staff at the University of Sydney and the targeted behaviour change was reduction in the use of single-use coffee cups.

Project ideas need not necessarily be original or something that has not been done before. The reason for this group's decision to work on such an issue was that they knew of another group in the university who had attempted to address this but who had to discontinue their efforts due to various issues. This group saw that they did not need to come up with new ideas to address the problem because there was already a solution for it – reusable cups.

Li Yang, Alexis O'Connor, and Ying Yue Chen realised the magnitude of the issue when they carried out their literature review on the topic. While they knew that single-use coffee cups were highly consumed in Australia, they did not realise that coffee cups had become the second-largest contributor to waste. They were also taken aback that people were generally unaware of the negative impacts of using single-use coffee cups and seemed unable to change their behaviour.

The aim of this project was to encourage the use of reusable coffee cups among their target community. To achieve this aim, the students created a campaign using posters, slogans, and logos to go onto coffee cups and an Instagram account. Collaborating with two cafés on the university campus, Ralph's Café and Courtyard Café, as well as the University of Sydney Union (USU), they carried out their campaign over the course of three days, in conjunction with USU x Sustainability Week.

Figure 5.3 The stamped coffee cups with the campaign slogan

Figure 5.4 The final drafts of the posters designed by the students

The first challenge in their project was at the material design stage. Wanting to make sure that their materials directly engaged with their target community, the students planned for their logos and slogans to be placed on single-use coffee cups to remind consumers to use reusable cups the next time they bought coffee. Their initial idea was to place a sticker of their campaign slogan on the single-use coffee cups. However, through the use of PDA, the students realised that the stickers were not reusable or environmentally-friendly. The students eventually pivoted to using a stamp instead (see Figure 5.3) as it had higher reusability and was less detrimental to the environment.

Another pivot this group made in their project was to use social media as a platform for their campaign materials instead of displaying their posters at the pay counter in the cafes (see Figure 5.4). This decision happened as a result of consultation with their collaborators about the design of their posters and realising that digitising their poster was more environmentally-friendly for their project.

Example 3: Bins for the future

"Bins for the Future" was led by Mariana Sáez Minchala and Chihiro Ohta who aimed to cultivate a habit of recycling among school children in Chile. Having previously taught at Manantial School in Santiago, Chile, Mariana wanted to conduct the project in this school to address the issue of students throwing away recyclable materials such as paper, cardboard, cans, and plastic bottles into general waste bins.

One of the challenges Mariana and Chihiro faced was finding an incentive to foster students' interest in the topic. In collaboration with the school, they decided to create a contest to design bins in order to engage the students with the topic. Their collaborator and school principal, Ms. Acantrio, was very supportive of their work and considered the project a great opportunity to raise awareness towards caring for the environment. The winners of the competition would receive school recognition for their designs and their designs would be turned into bins that would be installed and used across the school.

Mariana and Chihiro created three primary materials: a poster, a video, and a package of resources for teachers to use with the students. The poster, as we can see in Figure 5.5, was designed to promote the contest. Pictures, colours and phrases were used to explain what the contest was about and how to participate. Next, a video on practical tips to protect the environment was developed; this provided practical tips to students on how to recycle daily. Finally, they created a resource package for teachers (see Figure 5.6) to teach recycling principles with students in their lessons.

When designing materials for the project, Mariana and Chihiro used their experience in Sydney as part of the PDA. They noticed how

Figure 5.5 The poster for the bin designing contest

communications around recycling in Sydney were well crafted and provided valuable information which they could leverage for the project. Using PDA on the Australian-based recycling materials, the two of them tailored their content to fit the Chilean context and the school.

A common theme we see from these three examples is the vital role that collaborators play. Having collaborators that believed in the CREDIBLE approach made a difference to their projects. These collaborators spent time to help the students refine their materials to fit the context, to show them better ways to be environmentally-friendly in their approach, and to provide authorisation for activities like holding contests and putting up signs within the area.

In the next chapter, we will continue to explore more examples of successful collaborations within CREDIBLE projects for health and wellbeing.

Hablemos del Rol de las Personas en el Reciclaje
(Proyecto de Reciclaje para 3° y 4° Medio)

Estimadas profesoras y Estimados profesores,

Agradecemos su apoyo en la promoción de este proyecto. El presente documento tiene como objetivo guiar la presentación de la temática propuesta de reciclaje.

Esta actividad está planificada para 30 minutos aproximadamente, sin embargo, es posible acortar o alargar la actividad según se estime conveniente.

El objetivo principal de esta actividad es proporcionar conocimiento y generar conciencia sobre la importancia del reciclaje y la labor de personas para contribuir al cuidado del medio ambiente.

Además, se invita a los estudiantes a participar en el concurso de creación de un basurero ecológico para iniciar el proceso de reciclaje desde el colegio.

Agradecemos sus comentarios y sugerencias en la implementación de este proyecto.

Diapositiva 1: Hablemos del rol de las personas en el reciclaje

Diapositiva 2: Video sobre el efecto humano en la contaminación en Chiloé

Reproduzca el video presentado el cual explica el efecto humano en la contaminación del medio ambiente, el video es parte de la nota verde de 31 minutos. El video se puede reproducir al copiar el link en YouTube indicado bajo la fotografía.

Diapositiva 3: Hablemos del rol de las personas en el reciclaje

A partir de las siguientes preguntas presentadas inicie una conversación y/o debate con los estudiantes.

🔹 ¿Quiénes son los responsables de la contaminación en Chiloé? *Respuesta varían*, puede enfocarse tanto en la contribución de empresas como de personas locales.

🔹 ¿Ocurre esto en tu entorno? ¿Dónde? *Respuesta varían.*

Diapositiva 4: ¿Qué podemos hacer?

Reproduzca el video presentado el presenta consejos practico para reducir la cantidad de basura generada por los seres humanos. El video puede ser reproducido al copiar el link en YouTube indicado bajo la fotografía.

Diapositiva 5: Hablemos del rol de las personas en el reciclaje

A partir de las siguientes preguntas presentadas inicie una conversación y/o debate con los estudiantes

🔹 ¿Qué podemos hacer para reducir los residuos en casa? *Respuestas varían.* Se sugiere mencionar consejos prácticos el utilizar servilletas de tela, dar un segundo uso a envases plásticos, reducir la compra de alimentos que vengan en envases plásticos, utilizar bolsas reutilizables, composteras, etc.

🔹 ¿Cuál es la diferencia entre Reutilizar y Reciclar?

Si los estudiantes no están seguros, se puede mencionar las siguientes definiciones:

Reciclar: Utilizar residuos para crear nuevos productos.
Reusar: En vez de botar envases plásticos o de otro material, darles un nuevo uso.

🔹 ¿Qué cosas podemos reutilizar? *Respuestas varían.* Para dar una idea a los estudiantes, puede mencionar, envases plásticos, bolsas, ropa, cartón, papel (usario por ambos lados), etc.

🔹 ¿Qué cosas se pueden reciclar? *Respuestas varían.* Para dar una idea a los estudiantes, puede mencionar plástico, latas, metal, aparatos electrónicos, papel, etc.

Diapositiva 6: invitación concurso reciclaje

Diapositiva 7: Referencias de fuentes

*Recursos extra: Manual para la gestión ambiental en Establecimientos educacionales: residuos, energía y agua.
http://old.acee.cl/576/articles-58685 doc pdf.pdf

Manual de la casa verde: https://mma.gob.cl/wp-content/uploads/2017/08/Manual-casa-verde-Version-Final.pdf

Figure 5.6 The teaching resources developed by Mariana and Chihiro

6 CREDIBLE projects for health and wellbeing

Over the years, many of our students have chosen to address issues relating to health and wellbeing. Each of the examples in this chapter deals with different issues in health faced by different target communities. For an international resident in a foreign country, misinformation and poor communication strategies can impact that person's behaviour, leading them to avoid seeking out health services if they are sick or unwell. For local residents, this may be less of an issue, but living a healthy lifestyle might be more of a challenge in today's context where the nutritional quality of food consumed can impact one's health.

In the first project example, Wang Shuo Yang, Yuan Xin Er, and William Li drew on their experiences as international students navigating health policies in a foreign country. The second project example sees Kiahong Pan, Junzhe Li, Junyi Ye, and Zhihui Ren tackling an issue that was situated in their hometowns, one which they observed would affect the wellbeing of their community.

The CREDIBLE approach was instrumental in ensuring that the students worked across disciplines like nutrition and health communications, in particular, 'D' and 'I' which refer to 'Draws on an understanding of local knowledge and practices' and 'Informed by diverse approaches and experiences'. The students carried out 'D' through collaborations with their communities and stakeholders in the projects. The 'I' part of their project was in the form of literature and material review, which were not confined to only Applied Linguistics and academic sources, but health and medicine journals as well as real-world examples around them. By taking these steps, the students were able to successfully carry out interdisciplinary projects.

Finally, the third project example is the Trash Project. This project was first carried out by the entire intake of LNGS 7002 in 2018 and has since been expanded to include students in other units as well as contexts beyond the University of Sydney. Students working on this project drew on their knowledge of the linguistic landscape to investigate how transgressive signs can be used as an indicator of the health and environmental issues of people in various communities.

DOI: 10.4324/9781003495086-8

Example 1: Know your OSHC

Imagine being in a new country and needing to see a doctor because you've suddenly fallen sick. It can be quite confusing for new international students to figure out Australia's healthcare system, especially when they also need to adapt to other aspects of life in Sydney. Wang Shuo Yang noticed this issue when he first came to Australia in 2018. He was aware of the compulsory OSHC (Overseas Student Health Cover) that every student needed to obtain when they enrolled into university. However, he found the communication on OHSC was too generalised and infrequent, and the language used was confusing and unclear for international students. This, coupled with floating 'horror stories' of the high cost of ambulance services and long waiting periods, resulted in a fear of seeking medical help.

Wang Shuo Yang teamed up with Yuan Xin Er and William Li to launch an educational campaign targeting postgraduate international students at the University of Sydney. The campaign aimed to address the common misconceptions about OHSC and educate other international students on the medical services that are available to them with OHSC.

To prepare their materials, the students had to draw on the local understanding and practice of health services within Sydney. They collaborated with Sydney University Postgraduate Representative Association (SUPRA) to gain a better understanding of the types of challenges and misconceptions international students have around OSHC and health services in Sydney. Then, they surveyed the materials on OSHC available for international students and literature on health literacy and health behaviours. This allowed them to form an approach to the issue that was informed by diverse knowledge and experiences.

Figure 6.1 The final draft of the students' poster series design

68 Subaltern Linguistics

Their campaign consisted of three parts that function as a whole: posters, a brochure, and a website. The posters (see Figure 6.1) were designed to catch the attention of their target audience and lead them to the website; the brochure (see Figure 6.2) similarly points the readers to the website and offers more information; and the website,

Figure 6.2 The front and back of the brochure designed by the group

CREDIBLE projects for health and wellbeing   69

which contains even more information aimed to fill the knowledge gap of viewers and provide solutions to the issues that were identified by the three campaign organisers.

The material developed by these students is still available online and used by current students. This example shows how CREDIBLE projects create resources that can have a long lifespan and be useful to others.

Example 2: Reduce your sugar intake

This project aimed to raise awareness of the harms of added sugar and encourage children to reduce the consumption of sugar-sweetened beverages in Xia Yang Primary School, located in Xiamen City, Fujian Province, China. High sugar consumption leads to multiple health issues and reducing sugar intake can decrease the risk of associated health problems. This is one reason that many students in our classes focused on sugar and dietary issues.

In this project, Kiahong Pan, Junzhe Li, Junyi Ye and Zhihui Ren specifically wanted to tackle the issue of high consumption of milk tea among children. The group observed that popular brands of milk tea have high sugar content and include other processed ingredients.

Based in Sydney, the group communicated regularly with their collaborator at the primary school in Xiamen and this helped them draw on their collaborator's knowledge and expertise in teaching to align their material design with the needs of their target community. They also needed to understand the impacts of a high sugar diet on the health of children. To ensure they were passing on accurate information to the children, Kiahong Pan, Junzhe Li, Junyi Ye and Zhihui Ren conducted their literature review on nutritional health and childhood obesity. This required them to read beyond the applied linguistics journals and learn from other disciplines.

For their materials, the group designed two posters and one picture book. The poster introduced the project and gave instructions about the competition to the students. The picture book (see Figure 6.3)

Figure 6.3 Three pages from the children's picture book educating on the effects of consuming too many sweetened beverages

Figure 6.4 Some of the newspaper page designs by the students for the competition

served as a reference, delivering basic knowledge concerning sugary drinks which could be used by students during their design.

They also conducted a two-week pre-promotion and a one-week student design competition and received amazing and creative designs from the students. The competition where the students independently designed a handwritten newspaper page on reducing sugar intake resulted in beautiful artworks (see Figure 6.4) that were colourful, original (they did not simply copy the content of the picture book), and that showcased the children's understanding of the topic.

The CREDIBLE nature of this project helped Kiahong Pan, Junzhe Li, Junyi Ye and Zhihui Ren to adapt health information that was written for adults to primary school children. This allowed them to tackle the issue of high sugar consumption at the early stages of one's life, making the habit of consuming high sugar foods easier to break.

An important observation to note in both *Know Your OHSC* and *Reduce your sugar intake* is that students did not come up with the informational content themselves. They used principles in CREDIBLE and PDA to adapt the currently available information and make it relevant and appropriate for their target communities.

Example 3: The Trash Project

The Trash Project investigated how transgressive linguistic landscape – an example of which is trash – can be used as an indicator of the health and environmental issues of communities. Specifically, it aimed to address and take action on issues of health and environment.

There were eight groups of students who carried out this project in its first iteration. Each group was given the task of data collection through taking photos of trash within a 250-metre radius of the train

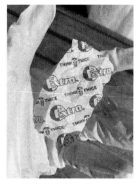

Figure 6.5 Picture of trash that shows the text clearly - text on the trash indicates that it is a gum wrapper

	SUMMARY:	Total No.:								
	DAY 2, AUGUST 18, 2018		Saturday							
No.	Code	Category	Sub-category	Item Description	Brand	Language on Item	Language of Item	Condition	Material	Waste Classification
113	C-18-092-1	Tobacco product	Cigarette box	Cigarette box	Rothman's	"Smoking causes	English	Clean and ripped	Cardboard and pl	Box: recyclable; pl
114	C-18-092-2	Tobacco product	Cigarette box	Cigarette box	Rothman's	"Smoking causes	English	Clean and ripped	Cardboard and pl	Box: recyclable; pl
115	J-46-093-1	Medical product	Alcohol swab	Alcohol swab pacl	Bodichek	Name, "Alcohol sw	English	Dirty	Paper	Non-recyclable
116	E-30-094-1	Receipt	Transportation	Train receipt		"Transport for NS\	English	Clean and crimple	Paper	Recyclable
117	E-30-095-1	Receipt	Transportation	Receipt for opal card top-up		"Customer copy",	English	Dirty	Paper	Recyclable
118	E-32-096-1	Receipt	ATM	St. George ATM receipt		"St George", date,	English	Dirty and crimpled	Paper	Recyclable
119	D-27-097-1	Reading material	Flyer	Flyer for health seminar		"coming to Conco	English	Dirty and crimpled	Paper	Recyclable
120	D-27-097-2	Reading material	Flyer	Flyer for health seminar		slogan, info about	English	Dirty and crimpled	Paper	Recyclable
121	E-32-098-1	Receipt	ATM	St. George ATM receipt		"St George", date,	English	Dirty and crimpled	Paper	Recyclable
122	E-32-099-1	Receipt	ATM	St. George ATM receipt		"St George", date,	English	Clean and crimple	Paper	Recyclable
123	L-100-1	Uncategorise		Desiccant		"Ever fresh", "do n	English and Japa	Dirty	Plastic	Non-recyclable
124	E-32-101-1	Receipt	ATM	St. George ATM receipt		"St George", date,	English	Dirty and crimpled	Paper	Recyclable
125	C-19-102-1	Tobacco product	Cigarette paper	Cigarette papers	Ventti	Name, "60 origina	English	Clean and crimple	Cardboard	Recyclable
126	C-19-102-2	Tobacco product	Cigarette paper	Cigarette papers	Ventti	"Featuring soft cor	English	Clean and crimple	Cardboard	Recyclable
127	A-14.1-103-1	Food	Condiment: sugar	Sugar packet	85 degrees	Name	English	Dirty and ripped	Waxed paper	Non-recyclable
128	A-1-104-1	Food	Candy	Mentos wrapper	Mentos	Name, flavour (mi	English	Clean, crimpled a	Plastic	Non-recyclable
129	A-1-105-1	Food	Candy	Mentos wrapper	Mentos	Name, flavour (mi	English	Clean, crimpled a	Plastic	Non-recyclable
130	A-5-106-1	Food	Gum	Extra wrapper	Extra	Name, "think twice	English	Dirty	Waxed paper	Non-recyclable
131	A-1-107-1	Food	Candy	Mentos wrapper	Mentos	Name, flavour (ora	English	Clean, crimpled a	Plastic	Non-recyclable
132	A-2-108-1	Food	Chocolate	Bueno wrapper	Kinder bueno	"White chocolate"	English	Clean and ripped	Plastic	Non-recyclable
133	A-5-109-1	Food	Gum	Extra wrapper	Extra	Name, "think twice	English	Dirty	Waxed paper	Non-recyclable
134	C-18-110-1	Tobacco product	Cigarette box	Cigarette box	Rothman's	"Smoking causes	English	Dirty and crimpled	Cardboard and pl	Box: recyclable; pl
135	C-18-110-2	Tobacco product	Cigarette box	Cigarette box	Rothman's	"Smoking causes	English	Dirty and crimpled	Cardboard and pl	Box: recyclable; pl
136	B-17.3-111-1	Beverage	Soft drink	Hungry Jack's sof	Hungry Jack's	"Hungry Jack's"	English	Clean	Plastic	Non-recyclable
137	L-112-1	Uncategorise		Coaster		"Jack Daniel's old	English	Clean	Cardboard	Recyclable
138	C-18-113-1	Tobacco product	Cigarette box	Cigarette box	Septwolves	"Septwolves", "[illegible]	English and Chin	Clean, crimpled a	Cardboard and pl	Box: recyclable; pl
139	C-18-113-2	Tobacco product	Cigarette box	Cigarette box	Septwolves	"Septwolves", "Ch	English and Chin	Clean, crimpled a	Cardboard and pl	Box: recyclable; pl
140	E-29-114-1	Receipt	Gambling	TAB receipt		Time and date, "b	English	Dirty, crimpled an	Paper	Recyclable
141	A-14.1-115-1	Food	Condiment: sugar	Sugar packet	Michel's patisseri	"Michel's"	English	Dirty and crimpled	Waxed paper	Non-recyclable
142	A-2-116-1	Food	Chocolate	Caramello wrappe	Cadbury's carame	"Caramello Koala"	English	Clean, crimpled a	Plastic	Non-recyclable
143	B-17.1-117-1	Beverage	NA: coffee	Hungry Jack's cof	Hungry Jack's	"Beans better...", "	English	Clean	Cardboard	Cup: non-recyclab
144	A-4-118-1	[illegible]	Fast food	Hungry Jack's par	Hungry Jack's	"Burgers are bette	English	Dirty and crimpled	Paper	Non-recyclable

Figure 6.6 Table with coding of the data and other relevant information

station in their suburb. They had to make sure the pictures they took showed the text on the trash clearly as in Figure 6.5.

Once the groups had collected their data, they began coding it by categorising it based on their analysis of the data. The data was then tabulated to include other important information on the trash such as brand, language of the text, nutritional content, and waste classification. For example, the gum wrapper we showed in Figure 6.5 is tabulated in Figure 6.6 at number 133, code A-5-109-1.

After coding the data, students were able to look for significant findings in their data and compare that with secondary data such as the demographic and health statistics of the suburbs which were collected from the Australian Bureau of Statistics and Healthstats.

The literature review for this project was crucial in helping the students understand and interpret the data they collected. In carrying out their literature review, students realised that their analysis was supported by other research that documents the correlation between socio-economic status and health. Their review of the literature also helped them identify the types of food that could lead to poor health outcomes such as the link between high fat, high sugar, and excessive consumption of alcohol with obesity. The students were able to use what they learnt from the literature in other disciplines and apply it to the categorising and coding of their data.

The final step in this project was taking action on the health and environmental issues found within the suburbs. The students wrote a list of recommendations, using their findings to provide evidence for the need to act.

This initial Trash Project has kickstarted other projects in different countries. For example, in May 2024, students in the Applied Linguistics program at Universitas Negeri Yogyakarta (UNY), Indonesia, spent two days carrying out the Trash Project in their area. They learnt ways to categorise trash (transgressive linguistic landscape) and to correlate it with health issues in their communities. The Trash Project has now become an adaptable model for others who are concerned about the health and environment of their neighbourhood and wish to carry out the project on their own. A draft step-by-step guide for doing this can be found on the Free Linguistics Conference website.

While the Trash Project seems to be mainly focused on health and wellbeing, some overlap does occur with environmental issues such as littering, plastic packaging, and eating habits that are not sustainable for the environment. Hence, this example can also be extended into using CREDIBLE for environmental issues.

Future considerations: endometriosis health campaign

From all of the examples we have seen so far, not only in this chapter but throughout the book, we can see how CREDIBLE is an integral approach to creating interdisciplinary projects. One of the authors of this book, Lee Cheng Koay is doing her PhD studies in applying CREDIBLE to a health campaign.

The target community for her project is teenage girls in Malaysia who could be living with endometriosis. Endometriosis is a health condition where the body grows the cells of the uterus in other places and organs that are not the uterus. This leads to symptoms such as pelvic pain commonly known as period cramps, fatigue, infertility, and irregular periods. Endometriosis is a common health condition around the world. It is thought that one in ten women globally have endometriosis.

Despite being a common condition, the diagnosis of endometriosis is often made in women in their thirties and forties, even though the signs and symptoms may already be present in earlier years. Lee Cheng herself was diagnosed in her early 30s. The delay in diagnosis can be detrimental to health outcomes because endometriosis is a condition that worsens over time if nothing is done to address it.

Lee Cheng's personal experience and concerns over the delay in diagnosis have motivated her to use her knowledge and expertise in health communication, as well as her background as an applied linguist, to tackle this issue in Malaysia, the country where she grew up. Her concern is for the population of girls and women in Malaysia who have to deal with stigma around taboo subjects like menstruation and endometriosis.

Using CREDIBLE, she will design and develop materials that will help its users to understand what endometriosis is and how they can find help and take action to manage this condition if positively diagnosed.

While this project is on-going and not yet completed, we include it in this chapter to share with you how we can use CREDIBLE to find solutions to issues that we ourselves may face. Through our CREDIBLE projects, we can empower our own communities to be better and healthier.

In the next chapter, we take a deep dive into a CREDIBLE project that empowers communities through economic development.

7 CREDIBLE projects for economic development

In this chapter, we exemplify what CREDIBLE projects for economic development can look like with a program called Language Travels. Taking language endangerment as a critical issue to address, Language Travels was pioneered by organisers of the Free Linguistics Conference, 2018, to enhance language maintenance efforts being made by the Kristang community members to strengthen the use and vitality of their language in Malacca, Malaysia.

The plight of endangered languages has been gaining attention within and outside the field of linguistics. There is a growing recognition that unless something is done urgently, more and more languages will continue to face extinction. Since each language is unique and captures one way in which people understand and engage with the world (as discussed in Part I of the book), a loss of language diversity implies a loss of our ways of understanding the world.

However, while an awareness of the urgency of maintaining linguistic diversity is increasing, there are few projects that have been shown to help achieve these goals. In addition, we have noticed that while colonial linguists continue to document and describe languages, these languages continue to weaken and die out. One reason for this is that language descriptions don't necessarily empower these languages – they are written in academic registers that are not even accessible to the members of the community. Another reason for this is that colonial linguists fail to realise that it is not the language that weakens or dies out, but rather it is the members of a community who are weak (because of dispossession, occupation, and/or colonisation) and unable to maintain their language. So, in many ways, to empower a language, we need to empower the community.

Language Travels was developed with an understanding that if we create a project that brings an economic incentive for the community members to maintain and strengthen their language, then they would do so. With this goal in mind, the Language Travels project brought a group of Language Travellers to the community, who paid their way to learn Kristang from the community members. This project was documented by Lee Cheng Koay in her MAK Halliday Gold

DOI: 10.4324/9781003495086-9

Medal-receiving Masters dissertation: Creating a language-based micro-economy through tourism and prestige planning: The case of Language Travels in Malacca.

Language Travels in Malacca (2018)

Language Travels is a language-based tourism program that was pioneered through the collaboration of the organisers of the Free Linguistic Conference (FLC) group, the Malaccan Portuguese Eurasian Association (MPEA), and some staff and students at the University of Malaya, Kuala Lumpur. The goal of the program was to use tourism to enhance the prestige of Indigenous languages by engaging and learning from the communities.

This program took place from 6 to 8 July 2018 in Malacca, Malaysia. The 3-day program was advertised on the FLC website as a pre-conference activity leading up to the 12th International Free Linguistics Conference in Kuala Lumpur, and was designed to immerse the participants in the culture and traditions of the Malaccan Portuguese community. The participants travelled to Malacca to learn Kristang and also learnt about other aspects of Kristang culture, architecture, history, and traditions (see Table 7.1 for the full itinerary of the program).

Table 7.1 Itinerary of the 3-day Language Travels program

Day 1: Friday, 6 July 2018	
10:00 am	Meet at the lobby of the Faculty of Languages & Linguistics, University of Malaya
10:30 am	Leave for Malacca
12:30 pm	Arrive at hotel, lunch and check-in
2:00 pm–5:30 pm	Language Workshop (20 min tea break at about 3:30 pm)
7:30 pm	Dinner at the Portuguese Settlement
Day 2: Saturday, 7 July 2018	
7:20 am	Leave hotel for walking tour
8:00 am	Walking tour of Malacca
12:00 noon	Leave for Chitty Village for lunch *(The Malacca Chitties are another creole community in Malaysia, apart from the Malacca Portuguese and the Malacca Baba)*
2:00 pm	Return to Portuguese Settlement
2:30 pm–5:30 pm	Language Workshop (20 min tea break)
Day 3: Sunday, 8 July 2018	
9:00 am–11:00 am	Practice session
11:00 am	Performance by participants
1:00 pm	Lunch
2:30 pm	Leave for Kuala Lumpur

Kristang in danger

Consisting of approximately 2150 mother-tongue speakers worldwide, speakers of Kristang can be found mainly in Malacca, Kuala Lumpur and Singapore. Kristang evolved in the 16th century, when the Portuguese arrived in Malacca, a location considered by many as strategic for trade, leading to the mingling and intermarrying of Portuguese settlers with the locals. The descendants of that community are those that inherit the language, Kristang.

Kristang is a Portuguese-based creole mixed with Malay, the national language of Malaysia. Kristang is endangered because it faces the threat of language shift to English and Malay. Malay, being the national language, is a mandatory subject in the local education system, and fluency in this language contributes towards academic success. In addition, English, as the language of globalisation, is used more often than Kristang in the community.

The socio-political context has also influenced this language shift. There is a perception among Malaysians that being fluent in English and Malay will help one achieve economic success, because of comparisons with the socio-economic status of other ethnic groups in Malaysia. Hence, there is a fear of being left behind, both in the political and economic sectors, which drives the language shift from Kristang to English and Malay. Furthermore, while the older generation hold on to Kristang as part of their identity of being a Malaccan Portuguese with pride, the younger generation tend not to.

Over the last few decades there has also been a decrease in the presence of Kristang in the family domain. This is partly because there are few community-friendly resources available that could aid in language maintenance. At the point when Language Travels was set up, language documentation of Kristang included a dictionary,

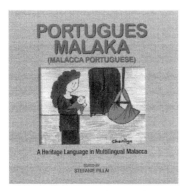

Figure 7.1 Cover of book 'Portugues Malaka' - a learning resource for Kristang developed by the local community in collaboration with Stephanie Pillai, one of the organisers of Language Travels

CREDIBLE projects for economic development

Figure 7.2 Participants and host community together at the end of Language Travels

a few linguistic descriptions, an online grammar resource, and an introductory learning resource (see Figure 7.1). However, despite having these resources and being in an environment where Kristang was spoken regularly, the younger generation were not fluent in the language.

Positive outcomes of Language Travels

Language Travels had a positive impact on the community in three major ways. The three areas of benefit were economic, building the prestige of the language, and a boost in the self-confidence of the children in the community. In this chapter, we will take a closer look at the first two benefits as they relate more strongly to the impact of economic development in this community.

1. Language Travels brought economic benefit

A key issue identified in literature on cultural tourism is the ways in which businesses exploit the local community by using their knowledge of the culture and their skills to offer services and products to tourists, keeping most of the profits for themselves and paying meagre wages to the local community. To address this issue, the organisers of Language Travels intentionally collaborated with the local community to identify skills and knowledge that could be turned into a direct source of income for the community (see Figure 7.2).

The total revenue generated from participant registration was a little over 15,000 MYR (approximately 3,145 USD). As part of the model of Language Travels to empower local communities, the organisers intentionally sought out local businesses within the community to ensure that as much revenue from the program would be channelled back to them. The expenses covered main meals at a locally-owned restaurant, tea-time snacks that were handmade by the people in the community, and visiting a historical site at one of the villages.

All of the activities, such as the language workshop and the walking tour, were facilitated by members of the community, and this meant that they could earn an income for the time and energy that they contributed to sharing their culture and language with the participants. Resources for the language workshop that were created by members of the community were also purchased as part of the program.

It was important that those involved received some monetary benefit from their use of Kristang as that helped achieve the goal of improving the prestige of the language in the eyes of the language users.

In addition, the community has been organising and running Language Travels independently of FLC since its first offering. The reiterations of the project add a regular source of revenue to the members of the community from teaching their own language – and, in doing so, the community also maintain and build the prestige of the language.

2. Language Travels improved the prestige of Kristang

Language maintenance is dependent on intergenerational transmission which can often be interrupted when another language is placed at higher value because of its usefulness to the language user. Hence, the language attitudes of a community can be negative if the language is only confined to the home domain. Language Travels uses the concept of improving language maintenance through changing language attitudes by introducing avenues for the host community to use Kristang beyond their homes and to earn an income.

Prestige planning is a form of language planning that focuses on improving the value of a language to a community. In Language Travels, the two ways in which the prestige of Kristang was impacted were through the generation of income with language-based activities (language workshops and historical site visits) and the actual learning of the language by participants of the program from language users.

While we are able to see how the creation of a micro-economy as described above helped to improve the prestige of Kristang, the contact of between participants and the host community also helped build the prestige of the language.

The Kristang language workshops were fun, engaging, and full of creative activities. These workshops did not involve learning the language through descriptions of grammar as one might observe in a typical classroom-style teaching. Kristang was taught by the children of

CREDIBLE projects for economic development

Figure 7.3 Some of the lyrics to Nina Boboi in Kristang with Malay and English translation published in the learning resource 'Nina Boboi'. The lyrics are accompanied by drawings from children in the community who have learnt the lullaby

the community through a lullaby known as 'Nina Boboi' (watch a recording of the launch of Nina Boboi here).

You can see parts of the lyrics of Nina Boboi represented in Kristang with Malay and English translation in Figure 7.3. The Kristang version with English translation was used in Language Travels because many of the Language Travellers were international visitors who did not know Malay. However, the inclusion of the Malay translation is important as it opens up Language Travels in the future to local communities who may engage with the program better if offered in Malay.

Through the process of watching the participants learn the lullaby, the community reported a sense of pride for their language, and a desire to see it shared outside of Language Travels. The quotes below from three elders in the community, Sara, Philomena and Michael, who collaborated with the organisers of Languages Travels exemplify this.

"I didn't know that you all are from different parts of the world. So, I am happy the Kristang has gone international, and please continue singing the song, and don't forget to sing the tune, okay? Continue singing and share it. If you have your students, share it with them and spread the word of us here." – Sara

"I think I am glad that we shared this with you. You are very warm, warm people and... bring these memories back with you all. Teach others about us so that it never dies. You know, our Kristang never dies." – Philomena

"We feel so – we feel good, you know, that we have done this, honestly. And to your question whether we want to go further than this, well why not? Because this has produced very positive results." – Michael

Another contributing factor to improving the prestige of Kristang is the identity of the participants of Language Travels themselves. The background of the participants varied widely, with participants from Australia, Brazil, China, Japan, Pakistan, Philippines, and other parts of Malaysia. As we saw in Sara's quote, seeing Kristang being sung by people from different parts of the world gave the host community pride that their language had "gone international" and was therefore worthy of learning and maintaining.

Other iterations of Language Travels

As we write this chapter, an ongoing effort to organise Language Travels in North Lombok, Indonesia is underway (see Figure 7.4). Building on the success of the first Language Travels, participants will immerse themselves in the Sasak language through interactive workshops and traditional performances. Having taken place on September 30 – October 2, 2024, the program incorporated cultural

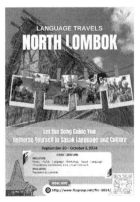

Figure 7.4 A flyer promoting Language Travels in North Lombok
Source: www.flcgroup.net/language-travels-2024/

village activities, provided insights into traditional crafts and Sasak lifestyles, and introduced participants to authentic Sasak cuisine, rich in unique flavours and cultural significance.

The North Lombok Language Travels was initiated by the FLC 2024 team, which includes a group of Sasak youth and community leaders who live in North Lombok. In developing the program, the North Lombok team is learning about their own language and culture. For example, they are learning the Aksaara, their Indigenous syllabic writing script that was replaced by a phonetic one during colonisation and occupation. The team is also creating a set of resources to learn and teach their mother tongue. In creating these resources, they are collaborating with their elders, academics at the local universities, Sasak musicians, and local artists. The team plans to continue offering Sasak language courses to other Language Travellers after the initial launch. They also have plans to publish the resources that they are developing through a local university press.

There are also other plans for Language Travels to make its way to China. These efforts are evidence of the successful nature of this model. Just as we have seen with the Trash Project, it is possible for these examples of CREDIBLE projects to be replicated in and adapted by different communities around the world.

Now as we move into Part III of this book, where you will learn how to do CREDIBLE projects, we hope that these examples from the chapters in Part II have inspired you to start thinking about the communities you belong to and how might you create a CREDIBLE project of your own.

Part III

How to create CREDIBLE projects

Part III of the book guides readers through the process of creating CREDIBLE projects, with a focus on practical application. It consists of three chapters: Chapter 8, Chapter 9, and Chapter 10.

In Chapter 8, we explicitly step through the four stages of creating a CREDIBLE project: conceptualisation, data analysis, material design, and action and continuity. This is done by using *The Ribbit-Ribbit Pond* picture book, designed by a former student of the Master of Applied Linguistics program from The University of Sydney, as a model. Each stage is broken down with detailed examples from the model text, highlighting key components of each CREDIBLE stage and demonstrating the processes involved.

Chapter 9 involves a collaborative effort in which readers will jointly create a CREDIBLE project, focusing on an environmental issue in a community of their choosing. In this chapter, we will use another student example on garbage sorting to provide guidance and support to tackle each stage effectively.

In Chapter 10, readers are given the opportunity to independently apply the knowledge and skills acquired in the previous chapters to develop their own CREDIBLE project. They will be guided by questions to ensure each stage is completed thoroughly and effectively, so a project report can be documented to share learning, successes and areas of improvement with others.

By the end of Part III, you will have a comprehensive understanding of the CREDIBLE approach and the ability to create meaningful projects that address real-world issues.

DOI: 10.4324/9781003495086-10

8 How do we do CREDIBLE? – *The Ribbit-Ribbit Pond*

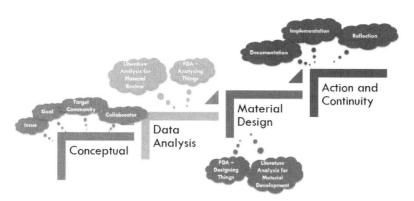

Figure 8.1 Stages of creating a CREDIBLE project

Conceptualisation

In the first stage of creating a CREDIBLE project (see Figure 8.1 above for an overview of the four stages of developing a CREDIBLE project), our main goal is to identify a problem or issue within a community and find effective ways to engage with that community. To make sure the project is relevant, we need to consult and involve community members at every step. This collaboration lays the groundwork for successful implementation and sustained impact, particularly in the final phase of Action and Continuity, in which community members play a pivotal role in executing and monitoring project progress.

After identifying the issue, we work with community members to set a clear and **achievable** goal. This goal should be realistic and based on:

- A community that we are part of or connected to;
- An understanding of the community's socio-semiotics;
- A reasonable timeframe;
- A budget and other resources, as necessary.

To illustrate the application of the four stages of a CREDIBLE project, we will delve into the analysis of *The Ribbit-Ribbit Pond*, which was

DOI: 10.4324/9781003495086-11

initially developed as an English-Spanish bilingual children's picture book authored by Ivan Ignacio Parra Gonzalez. This project was also introduced in Chapter 2 of the book.

Questions to think about in the conceptualisation stage

- What is the issue/problem you want to address?
- What is the expected impact of this project? Who will benefit from this project and how?
- Who is the target community?
- What is the goal of the project? Is it achievable?
- Who are the relevant stakeholders/collaborators?
- Why do you want to do this project?
- What is the expected timeline of this project?

The Ribbit-Ribbit Pond

The Ribbit-Ribbit Pond (Figure 8.2) is a bilingual children's picture book authored by Ivan Ignacio Parra Gonzalez as part of the Master of Crosscultural and Applied Linguistics program at the University of Sydney. A copy of Ivan's dissertation can be found here: www.academia.edu/49674264/The_Making_of_the_Ribbit_Ribbit_Pond_Nurturing_Childrens_Intercultural_Communicative_Competence_through_a_CREDIBLE_Project. The book was written in the context of

Figure 8.2 The Ribbit-Ribbit Pond

Chile's changing demographics as migrants from Haiti who do not speak Spanish migrate to Chile. In his Masters Dissertation, Ivan speaks of his first-hand experience as a teacher witnessing other teachers labelling newly arrived Haitian students as "less educated" as they had emigrated from a poorer country than Chile and did not speak Spanish. Ivan also observed that there were few resources or initiatives to support the migrant community.

To help address the negative perception of migrants in Chile, especially in schools, Ivan's goal was to design a bilingual English-Spanish picture book which would foster positive attitudes towards migration and multilingualism, with the ultimate goal of nurturing children's intercultural competence. The target audience and community in focus were teachers, students and parents, migrants and non-migrants. The book included reflection questions at the end for adults reading to children to consider and discuss together. Being a member of the community, Ivan had first-hand experience of the negative attitudes towards newly arrived migrants in Chile. To develop and design the picture book, Ivan collaborated with his supervisor and an illustrator over several months. Recently, Ivan's book has been published.

The Ribbit-Ribbit Pond exemplifies a CREDIBLE project, aiming to tackle a real-world issue and foster positive change. Unlike typical academic work that often prioritises Western theories and marginalises non-Western perspectives, CREDIBLE projects focus on empowering communities to address the real problems they face. This chapter will illustrate this approach by using *The Ribbit-Ribbit Pond* as an example, highlighting the core principle of collaboration with communities at the heart of CREDIBLE projects.

Activity 1

1. What is the issue/problem that aims to be addressed through the creation of *The Ribbit-Ribbit Pond* picture book?
2. What is the goal of this book?
3. Who are the target audience of the book? Think about the community the book is set in, and who will be reading the book.
4. Who will benefit from this book?
5. Who were the collaborators in the creation of the book?
6. Why was this book created?

Data analysis

The second stage of developing a CREDIBLE project is the data analysis stage where we conduct a literature analysis and a project review. The purpose of the data analysis stage is to conduct research on the issue, gather information on the target community, and also identify similar projects that have addressed the issue, either in the target community or elsewhere. We need to collect as much information as possible about the inception of these projects, the materials developed, how community stakeholders were engaged, and whether the projects were successful in addressing the issue, and why. To determine if past projects were successful, we need to establish whether their goals were achieved. The best indicator of success is whether the community has changed its behaviour. For example, Chapter 3 demonstrated how Australia's National Tobacco Campaign achieved its goal as it has been successful in reducing cigarette smoking rates in Australia over a 20-year period. When carrying out project reviews, ensure you can find evidence that there has been positive change in the community since the project's implementation. We can learn from these past projects to inform our own project design.

There are many ways to conduct research. We can search the internet, looking at news websites, organisation and community websites, academic articles, and more. We can also engage with communities who have designed similar projects, or anyone who can give us insights, ideas, and inspirations for the design of our own projects. It is by engaging with communities and being hands-on that sets subaltern linguistics and the CREDIBLE project approach apart from typical academic applied linguistics work.

To develop and carry out successful CREDIBLE projects, it is crucial to identify, study, and learn from similar or related projects. But how do we do this in a systematic manner to ensure the success of our own projects? This is why broad Positive Discourse Analysis (PDA) was developed as an analytical tool, as it focuses on understanding how successful texts and materials work to create new projects.

As discussed in Chapter 3, the aim of PDA is to analyse as well as design materials that improve / will improve our communities. This approach complements Critical Discourse Analysis (CDA), which typically studies how power operates in and through hegemonic texts. In subaltern education, we extend the idea of looking at positive examples by examining how a project interacts with all our sensory systems (see Chapter 2).

There are two broad PDA tools: one for analysing successful projects and another for designing new ones. Below, we introduce the broad PDA form for analysing successful projects and in a later section we explain the PDA form for designing projects. Using these forms will help us in developing our CREDIBLE projects.

Table 8.1 presents the PDA-analysing things form. "Things" refers to any successful project or material you are analysing, such as a poster, video, or program. If you are analysing a campaign or program with multiple materials, fill out one form per material. When presenting your

Table 8.1 PDA-Analysing Things Form

INSERT MATERIAL

Name the thing:

Describe the thing:

Is this part of a larger campaign/project/program:

If yes, what other materials are part of the campaign? Provide an overview of materials included in the campaign and highlight which things you will analyse. Include a reason for your decision.

What are the goals of the thing?

Context and details about the thing:

- Who created it?
- Why was it created?
- Where was it created?
- When was it created?

Is there any other necessary information about the material?

Why do you think this thing is successful?

	Description	What meanings are being projected?
Sight		
Sound		
Smell		
Touch		
Taste		

PDA-analysing things form, insert your material for analysis in the INSERT MATERIAL section. For a video, embed the video or insert a link, and include some still images. The first set of questions relate to the contextual information about the material you are analysing, such as its purpose, goal, and why you think it is successful. This is followed by an analysis of the senses used or evoked in the material and the kinds of meanings they project. To illustrate how to carry out a broad PDA analysis, we will analyse *The Ribbit-Ribbit Pond*.

Questions to think about in the data analysis stage

- What has previously been done to address this issue? Was it in the target community or elsewhere?
- What kind of materials were designed for the project? Posters, activities, videos, books, guidelines, policies, economies etc.
- Based on your research, were the projects successful in addressing the issues? Why/why not?
- Which successful material(s) do you want to analyse in your broad PDA?

The Ribbit-Ribbit Pond

The development and design of *The Ribbit-Ribbit Pond* was informed by some key theories and approaches, namely the CREDIBLE approach to project design and intercultural communicative competence. As discussed previously, the CREDIBLE approach focuses on addressing real world issues, producing contextually relevant materials and resources, and engaging with local stakeholders. Table 8.2, completed by Ivan Parra Gonzalez, illustrates how the picture book embodies the principles of the CREDIBLE approach.

Ivan uses some useful theories to inform the development and design of *The Ribbit-Ribbit Pond*, including multimodality, translanguaging, narrative structure and genre theory, and Intercultural Communicative Competence. Briefly, multimodality posits that communication and meaning-making occur through multiple modes – such as text, images, audio, and gestures – rather than relying solely on language. It emphasises the interplay between these various modes to convey complex messages and enhance understanding. This is applied in *The Ribbit-Ribbit Pond* by using images and language together to convey complex ideas and emotions around migration and acceptance.

Aligning closely with multimodality are the theories of narrative structure and genre. Genre theory posits that all texts have a unique structure that tells us what the text is about i.e. what is happening, and who is involved in the text. In the case of *The Ribbit-Ribbit Pond* picture book, it has a narrative structure which involves aligning the verbal and visual modes of a story according to stages of orientation, complication, and resolution, with each containing different phases that interact to enhance the overall meaning and engagement.

Another key theory used to develop the picture book is that of translanguaging in education which refers to the practice in which students use their full linguistic repertoires, creatively drawing on multiple languages as integrated systems, to enhance participation, agency, and linguistic confidence in the classroom. This closely links to the theory of Intercultural Communicative Competence (ICC) which

Table 8.2 A CREDIBLE analysis of *The Ribbit-Ribbit Pond*. Source: Ivan's dissertation

Contextually relevant: Chile has always been a country that receives a high number of immigrants from other Latin American countries due to its solid economy and better standard of living. In recent years, however, immigration from Haiti has started to change the linguistic landscape of the country. In addition to language difference, the physical appearance of Haitian people is quite different from the appearance of Chilean people, which has led to a number of cases of racism and xenophobia. The development of intercultural communicative competence, therefore, has become extremely necessary in Chilean society in order to guarantee not only a safe, welcoming space for immigrants, but also a more tolerant society that respects the differences of the different cultural groups already coexisting in the country.

Responds to practical needs: parents and teachers need resources to nurture intercultural competence in children. On the one hand, reading stories to children is a valued activity in the Western world, especially in English-speaking countries. Noticeably, these countries receive high numbers of immigrants every year, hence the need for families to discuss this issue and prepare children to be competent intercultural communicators, which can be done through a fun, educative activity such as reading a storybook. On the other hand, there is a lack of EFL materials explicitly designed to build students' intercultural communicative competence, let alone on the topic of immigration. What is more, most of the existing materials do not foster multilingualism, but only the target language, i.e. English. Consequently, what I tried to achieve was the development of a learning resource with simple language that English learners in Spanish-speaking countries can easily understand, and that values multilingualism in both in the content of the story and in the design of the book itself.

Engages stakeholders: in order to create a good-quality book, this project needed the collaboration of an experienced illustrator. Once the book is finished, I will contact a publishing house to put it out so that parents and schools can have access to it.

Draws on understanding of local knowledge and practices: telling stories is a powerful tradition in which adults not only entertain children, but also transmit values and knowledge of the world to them. Consequently, using this traditional practice to educate children about immigration can be very fruitful as a number of positive attitudes can be nurtured in children through a well-written story.

Informed by diverse approaches and experiences: the development of intercultural communicative competence through literature has long been recognised by researchers (see, for example,

Rodríguez and Puyal, 2012; Volkmann, 2015; Nie, 2017; and Magos, 2018), hence the selection of this methodology for my project. In addition, the creative process behind the book was guided by different theories related to the development of intercultural communicative competence, the valuing of multilingualism, and the use of social semiotic resources to convey meanings. The appropriate design of the images was crucial to the project, as my experience suggests kids love to look at the drawings of storybooks and try to make sense of them even if they have not reached a good level of literacy.

Benefits local communities: the book is intended to benefit every kid that gets their hands on it. Because the book is being produced with Chilean children in mind, the book is intended to prepare Chilean children for their future multicultural encounters. But the book is not meant to be published only in Chile; as I am currently living in Australia, my purpose is to also publish it here so that Australian children can benefit from this story. Furthermore, the fact that *The Ribbit-Ribbit Pond* is a multilingual resource makes it possible to reach a broader global audience of people who can speak, or want to learn, either Spanish or English.

Leads the field/discipline and contributes to the larger global theories: *The Ribbit-Ribbit Pond* addresses the development of intercultural communicative competence, an issue that has gained a great deal of attention from researchers during recent decades. The book, however, intends to be a practical application of the existing findings on the topic in connection with foreign language education. On top of this, the book has been designed in consideration of the tenets of translanguaging, a language theory that is relatively new in Applied Linguistics and which still needs to receive a great deal of attention from researchers. In fact, the construction of pedagogical resources attending to translanguaging is one of the research areas that needs further development; herein lies the originality and pioneering nature of my project, as I have engaged in that endeavour.

Ethical: the ethical aspect of this project lies in its main purpose, which is nurturing a positive attitude towards immigration in children while promoting the development of their identities as multilingual speakers. This project does not harm or take advantage of people to reach its goal; instead, it simply seeks to cultivate tolerance, empathy, and love in the citizens of tomorrow, who will engage in the eradication of discrimination against immigrants and refugees.

relates to the ability of people to interact with those of other cultures and language backgrounds. Furthermore, the theory posits that our attitudes, i.e. the way we feel about things/people, are a fundamental starting point for the development of intercultural communicative competence, followed by our knowledge and skills.

Using the concept of ICC, Parra Gonzalez states "the attitudes of respect, openness, and curiosity and discovery are implicitly transmitted to the readers of the book through the alignment of its verbal and visual modes" (p. 54). This is all with the aim of fostering positive attitudes towards Haitian migrants and other migrants in Chile, especially those who do not speak Spanish.

Table 8.3 provides a broad PDA-analysing things analysis of *The Ribbit-Ribbit Pond*. The PDA analysis provides an analysis of pages 12 and 22 and the sensory analysis provides some main ways in which the five senses are evoked in the book. Depending on which material(s) are being analysed, the PDA – analysing things form can be more detailed, and as mentioned previously, if more than one material is being analysed, it is a good idea to also explain how the different

---

Table 8.3 PDA Analysis of *The Ribbit-Ribbit Pond*

Name the thing: *The Ribbit-Ribbit Pond* picture book

Describe the thing: The book tells the story of a group of frogs who arrive at a new pond. The frogs look and sound different to the existing frogs. However, when the existing frogs start to interact with the new frogs, they find they have a lot in common and welcome the new frogs to the pond.

Is this part of a larger campaign/project/program: No

If yes, what other materials are part of the campaign? Provide an overview of materials included in the campaign and highlight which things you will analyse. Include a reason for your decision.

What are the goals of the thing? To foster intercultural competence and embrace cultural diversity among its readers.

Context and details about the thing:

- **Who created it?** Ivan Ignacio Parra Gonzalez
- **Why was it created?** It was created as part of his Masters Dissertation
- **Where was it created?** It was created in Sydney, Australia
- **When was it created?** 2021

Why do you think this thing is successful? The book is aimed at children, parents and educators, and promotes positive attitudes towards migrants in a simple story easily understood by small children. The book also provides reflection activities at the end for adults to engage the children.

Is there any other necessary information about the material?

	Description	What meanings are being projected?
Sight	Writing in English and Spanish; pictures; bright and bold colours	The pictures reinforce what is written, making it easy for children to follow. The bright and bold colours create a sense of positive attitude.
Sound	Onomatopoeia	The book provides the different sounds the two groups of frogs make which can be sounded out.
Smell	Natural landscape	While the sense of smell is not obvious; the various landscape pictures can evoke smell of nature.
Touch	Rain; sunshine	The book describes the new frogs' journey through rain and sun, evoking these sensations for the readers.
Taste	Food	The book explains that frogs in the pond enjoy the same food demonstrating that food can bring different people together.

materials work together and interact with each other as part of the overall campaign, project or program.

Activity 2

Based on the contextualisation of *The Ribbit-Ribbit Pond* so far, conduct your own research on the migration situation in Chile. Consider the migrants' countries of origin, their mother tongues, their experiences upon settling in Chile, and the challenges they face.

Additionally, research what has been done in Chile to address the language barriers that migrants, especially young children, encounter. You can also expand your search to include other South American countries facing similar situations or you can focus on your own country/region.

Activity 3

In this activity, refer to Figure 8.3 and think about why you think this page from *The Ribbit-Ribbit Pond* fits in with the overall aim of the picture book to foster positive attitudes towards migrants.

Then we will practice conducting a sensory analysis. Refer to Figure 8.3 again, and complete Table 8.4.

How do we do CREDIBLE?   95

Figure 8.3 Images from *The Ribbit-Ribbit Pond*

Table 8.4 The five material senses

	Description	What meanings are being projected?
Sight		
Sound		
Smell		
Touch		
Taste		

Material design

In the previous section, we conducted a literature review and broad PDA analysis of *The Ribbit-Ribbit Pond*. Analysing successful materials and projects is the first step in designing your own. This helps you understand why these materials or projects have achieved their goals, so you can apply these insights to your own design. The broad PDA-designing things form is the next step after analysing successful materials or projects. As shown in Table 8.5, the PDA-designing things form is similar in format to the PDA-analysing things form, but the questions are now focused on what you need to consider when designing your materials. This form is intended to guide your material design and should be completed before you start designing. Once completed, insert your material in the [INSERT MATERIAL DESIGN] section. If you have created a video, include still images as well.

Table 8.5 PDA-Designing Things form

INSERT MATERIAL DESIGN

Names:

Project title:

Goal/outcomes of the project (what do you hope to achieve)?

Where will you be carrying out this project? Give details about the context (including people using the materials)

Significance of the project (why is it important to do this)?

Material/activity development (what will be created)?

What things/readings/projects have you analysed in developing your work? What were some key observations?

Alignment between design and goals (how do you expect to achieve your goals based on what you will do?

What are some of the challenges that you may face in developing and/or implementing your project?

What are some potential negative consequences of the project and how can you avoid/minimise these?

Which material senses will your thing/project utilise? How?

(Complete the table below for each thing you plan to create)

	Description	What meanings are being projected?
Sight		
Sound		
Smell		
Touch		
Taste		

The questions in the form help you consider the importance of your design and how to create materials that align with your goals. This is followed by the material senses table, which encourages you to think about how to utilise sensory elements in your design. You can use this

How do we do CREDIBLE?   97

form during the conceptualisation stage to help you think about the goals, target community, and significance of your project.

Questions to think about in the material design stage

- Does your material design align with your goal? Will it address the issue you sought to address?
- How will you use the multiple sensory systems (either explicitly or metaphorically) in your design?
- How will your stakeholders be involved in the material design?

The Ribbit-Ribbit Pond

The PDA-designing things form in Table 8.6 below provides an example of how the form is to be filled out prior to designing materials for a CREDIBLE project.

Table 8.6 The Ribbit-Ribbit Pond – designing things

INSERT MATERIAL DESIGN

Names: Ivan Parra Gonzalez

Project title: *The Ribbit-Ribbit Pond*

Goal/outcomes of the project (what do you hope to achieve)? The goal is to foster positive attitudes towards migrants in Chile and build intercultural communicative competence.

Where will you be carrying out this project? Give details about the context (including people using the materials) The Book will be developed in Australia as part of a Master's dissertation with the aim of publishing the book in Chile

Significance of the project (why is it important to do this)? Many migrants from Haiti have been migrating to Chile, and these migrants often do not speak Spanish. Parents and children are not given the support they need to adapt to their new home. It is thus important to foster positive attitudes towards migrants/migration in young children so they become more accepting of those who look and speak "differently" to them.

Material/activity development (what will be created)? A children's picture book

What things/readings/projects have you analysed in developing your work? What were some key observations? Theories state that a fundamental starting point for building intercultural communicative competence are the attitudes we have towards others. The picture book will engender positive attitudes towards those who look "different" to "us".

Alignment between design and goals (how do you expect to achieve your goals based on what you will do?) It is hoped that the picture book along with the reflection questions at the end of the book will help foster positive attitudes towards migrants

What are some of the challenges that you may face in developing and/or implementing your project? Finding someone to design the illustrations and finding a publisher for the book

What are some potential negative consequences of the project and how can you avoid/minimise these? It is possible that some reading the book might feel judged. This is why the story will be about a group of frogs settling in a pond with existing frogs to ensure no one feels judged.

Activity 4

From the form in Table 8.7 complete the final question of the PDA-designing things form. What material senses do pages 5 and 6 of *The Ribbit-Ribbit Pond* book utilise to achieve its goal?

Table 8.7 The five material senses in *The Ribbit-Ribbit Pond*

Which material senses will your thing/project utilise? How? (Complete Table 8.7 for each thing you plan to create)

	Description	What meanings are being projected?
Sight		
Sound		
Smell		
Touch		
Taste		

Action and continuity

Once you have completed the PDA-designing things form and designed your material, activity, or program, it is time to implement your project in the community. Collaborate with your team and stakeholders to develop an implementation plan. The first step is to have community stakeholders review and approve the material design. Depending on your project, you might need to conduct a focus group to pilot the materials or activities with some community members. This helps determine if the materials align with your goals and if any adjustments are needed before full implementation.

Next, establish an implementation date or timeline. Consider whether there are events that might "overshadow" the implementation and how to raise awareness of your project. Once the project is implemented in the community, a key aspect of a CREDIBLE project is documentation. This includes both PDA forms and an evaluation of the project implementation. In the evaluation, describe how the project was carried out and how it was received by the community. Measure the project's impact by conducting interviews with community members and observing behavioural changes related to the issue. The documentation format will depend on the nature of the project. It could be a portfolio of everything that was done, a video, a written report, or another format. This documentation can then be handed over to the community to continue implementing and monitoring the project's outcomes. It can also serve as a resource for other communities facing similar issues.

Questions to think about in the action and continuity stage

- Will the community respond positively to the materials/project?
- When is an appropriate time to implement the project? Are there big events happening in the community?
- How do we evaluate the project's success? Is the issue still present in the community? Is it to the same degree as pre-implementation?
- How do we document and handover the project to the community? What is the best format to share what has been done?
- How can we continuously improve the project?

The Ribbit-Ribbit Pond

The Ribbit-Ribbit Pond was released in July 2024 by Starfish Bay Children's Books. With the publication of this book, Ivan has taken action and implemented his project. Additionally, translations of *The Ribbit-Ribbit Pond* are now available in 35 languages on the Free Linguistics Conference website. These translations have been adapted

100 Subaltern Linguistics

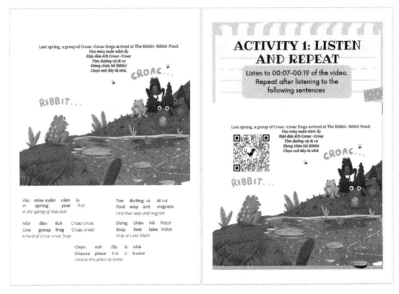

Figure 8.4 Activity from Vietnamese workbook *The Ribbit-Ribbit Pond*

Figure 8.5 Images from *The Ribbit-Ribbit Pond*

Figure 8.6 QR code from Vietnamese workbook of *The Ribbit-Ribbit Pond*

Figure 8.7 QR code from Chinese workbook of *The Ribbit-Ribbit Pond*

into workbooks for children, featuring activities based on the book as illustrated in Figures 8.4 and 8.5. The Vietnamese and Chinese workbooks include QR codes (Figures 8.6 and 8.7) that readers can scan to listen to the book being read on YouTube, facilitating the completion of the activities.

9 Let's do CREDIBLE together – taking care of the environment

Conceptualisation

Environmental sustainability is a significant challenge impacting many communities. In Chapter 5, we discussed three examples: garbage sorting, single-use coffee cups, and recycling. In this chapter, we will focus on the 'Garbage Sorting' project to illustrate the four stages of a CREDIBLE project, providing you with a practical guide for your own environmental initiatives.

The Garbage Sorting project was developed by Xinyi Zhang, Chu Yuan, Changyao Fang, and Yuelin Feng as part of their Masters in Crosscultural and Applied Linguistics program at The University of Sydney. As previously mentioned, students in this course created CREDIBLE projects to address issues within their target communities, with a strong focus on environmental problems. This real-world example offers practical insights and guidance as you navigate each stage of your own project.

The first stage of developing their CREDIBLE project was the conceptualisation stage, in which they identified the community they aimed to assist and pinpointed the specific environmental issues at hand (see Figure 9.1). The students selected the residential community of Li Hu Ming Xuan, where one of the students resided and observed that residents were not sorting their rubbish correctly and lacked proper instructions on how to sort garbage into the appropriate bins (e.g., food waste, recycling, etc.). Their goal was to educate both adults and children in the residential building about the city's garbage sorting system by developing tailored materials for each group. Addressing this issue was crucial for fostering a sustainable, clean, and liveable community.

To bring their project to life, they collaborated with the strata manager, who was involved in all aspects of the Li Hu Ming Xuan community and could assist them in reaching their target audience. Through the strata manager, they gained access to a WeChat group, allowing direct communication with residents. Additionally, one group member worked part-time at the local language school, providing direct access to the children in the community.

DOI: 10.4324/9781003495086-12

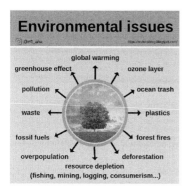

Figure 9.1 Example of environmental issues

Activity 5

In this activity, it's your turn to identify an environmental issue facing a community you would like to help, such as a workplace, village, school, apartment building, etc. Ensure that you will be able to reach the members of this community. If the community is too large (e.g., a city), your project might not be achievable. Once you've done this, consider your goal. What do you aim to achieve with your CREDIBLE project? Ensure your goal is realistic by focusing on a manageable target community and setting an achievable objective such as the goal identified in the Garbage Sorting project.

To help you conceptualise your project, answer the following questions and include any other relevant information:

- What is the issue/problem you want to address?
- What is the goal of the project? Is it achievable?
- Who is the target community?
- Who are the relevant stakeholders/collaborators?
- Why do you want to do this project?
- What are some of the resources that you may need to carry out this project?
- What is the expected impact of this project? Who will benefit from this project and how?
- What is the expected timeline of this project?

Data analysis

As explained in Chapter 8, the second stage of a CREDIBLE project is data analysis. In this stage, we conduct a literature analysis and project review to understand the context around our issue and to explore similar projects.

In their Garbage Sorting project, the group conducted an extensive literature review on the issue, dividing their research into three main areas:

- Government policies regarding garbage sorting;
- Social marketing theories;
- Similar campaigns on littering/garbage sorting.

Government policies informed the group about the garbage classification system (e.g., recycling, food waste, general waste), ensuring they had accurate and up-to-date information for the material design. By reviewing social marketing theories, they gained insights into designing materials aimed at behaviour change and how these approaches differ for adults and children. Lastly, reviewing similar campaigns aimed at encouraging proper rubbish disposal gave the group ideas for the different types of materials they could design for their target community.

In addition, the group consulted with their collaborator and made their own observations regarding garbage sorting. For example, they noted that there were no clear labels or instructions on the bins or walls indicating where to dispose of recyclables, general garbage, or kitchen waste, as illustrated in Figure 9.2. They also observed that the existing information related to garbage disposal focused on behaviours that endangered public health (e.g., "Do not throw rubbish out of the window") rather than on garbage sorting.

In addition to reviewing the literature and existing projects on garbage sorting, the group identified material they could use as a model for their own material development. Once they selected their model material, they conducted a broad PDA-analysing things form. This process helps us determine how well the model incorporates the five

Figure 9.2 Bins in Li Hu Ming Xuan before this project was implemented

Figure 9.3 Example of garbage sorting

material senses. By conducting a broad PDA, we can determine the extent to which the model has incorporated the material senses. If the model is lacking in using the five material senses, we can note this down and incorporate these elements into our design. In addition, it is useful to review multiple models and conduct PDA on these to strengthen the design of our own projects.

Figure 9.3 provides an example of a poster created to educate the public about garbage sorting. Table 9.1 exemplifies why this poster can serve as an example for our environmental project and how it utilises the five material senses to convey meanings. Notice how the poster uses the material senses both directly (e.g., sight) and indirectly/metaphorically (e.g., sound, touch, and smell) to communicate the importance of sorting rubbish into appropriate bins.

Activity 6

Now that you have identified an environmental issue facing a community, it is time to conduct a literature review on the issue. Begin by researching the issue within your specific community. Look for newspaper articles, videos, academic articles, or even social media posts where people are discussing the issue or raising awareness about it. Do they provide reasons for the issue? What can you or your collaborator observe about the issue? What can you see, hear, and feel? This comprehensive understanding will help inform your approach and ensure that your project is well-grounded in previous research and community-specific insights.

Table 9.1 PDA analysis of waste sorting poster

INSERT MATERIAL

Name the thing: waste sorting poster

Describe the thing: the poster illustrates in which bins to dispose rubbish

Is this part of a larger campaign/project/program: no

If yes, what other materials are part of the campaign? Provide an overview of materials included in the campaign and highlight which things you will analyse. Include a reason for your decision.

What are the goals of the thing? The poster aims to educate the public on how to dispose of different waste products correctly.

Context and details about the thing:

- Who created it?
- Why was it created?
- Where was it created?
- When was it created?

Is there any other necessary information about the material?

Why do you think this thing is successful? Using images in the poster means both children and adults can learn how to dispose of waste correctly

	Description	What meanings are being projected?
Sight	The poster provides examples of each waste type and their corresponding bin colour	This makes it easy for consumers to identify the correct bin for the waste products
Sound	While sound is not used directly, the images evoke the different sounds produced by different waste products	By evoking the sense of sound, this can aid consumers to dispose of waste correctly
Smell	The organic waste bin displays images of food products	This evokes the sense of smell associated with organic food waste, creating an association between the bin and its colour
Touch	Nil	Nil
Taste	The organic waste bin displays images of food products	This evokes the taste associated with organic food waste, creating an association between the bin and its colour

Activity 7

In this activity, conduct a project review to inform you of what has been done previously to address the issue, either in your community or elsewhere. A key aspect of conducting a project review is to identify the impact the project has had on the target community, helping to determine if it achieved its goals and was successful. When reviewing these projects consider the following questions:

Table 9.2 PDA-analysing things form

INSERT MATERIAL

Name the thing:

Describe the thing:

Is this part of a larger campaign/project/program:

If yes, what other materials are part of the campaign? Provide an overview of materials included in the campaign and highlight which things you will analyse. Include a reason for your decision.

What are the goals of the thing?

Context and details about the thing:

- Who created it?
- Why was it created?
- Where was it created?
- When was it created?

Is there any other necessary information about the material? Why do you think this thing is successful?

	Description	What meanings are being projected?
Sight		
Sound		
Smell		
Touch		
Taste		

- What was the aim of the project? What did the project aim to achieve?
- What materials were developed as part of the project? E.g. videos, posters, activities, books, workshop etc.
- How was the project implemented?
- What was the impact of the project? Was it successful or unsuccessful? How do you know if a project was successful or unsuccessful? What indicators demonstrate the success of the project?

Once you have completed your project review, choose a model project, material, or campaign, and complete the PDA – analysing things form in Table 9.2. When filling out the material senses table, consider how the material uses or evokes the senses to convey meanings related to the issue.

For sight, think about how writing, images, colours, graphics, etc., are used to communicate meanings. If you are analysing a purely visual material such as a poster or book, consider how the visual medium evokes the other senses. Do they use images of food, smoke, traffic, or dirt to evoke the senses of taste, smell, sound, and touch respectively? If you are analysing a video or a material that includes audio, consider the different sounds you can hear and the meanings they convey. For example, can you hear people talking, music, cars, etc.? Apply the same analysis to the other senses.

This detailed analysis will help you understand how effective the model is in using sensory inputs to communicate its message, and it will guide you in designing your own materials.

Material design

The students involved in the Garbage Sorting project created different materials for their two target audiences: a colouring book for children and posters for adults. The colouring book is illustrated in Figure 9.4, and the posters are illustrated in Figure 9.5. To guide the design of these materials, the group completed a PDA-designing things form for each design. Table 9.3 demonstrates the PDA-designing things form for the posters designed for the residents of the building. Notice that the group explicitly indicates the language of the material designs will be Cantonese, given that most residents speak Cantonese. This is a crucial consideration for your own project.

Activity 8

Having completed the PDA analyses on the materials we plan to use as models, we are now ready to start designing the materials for our

Let's do CREDIBLE together

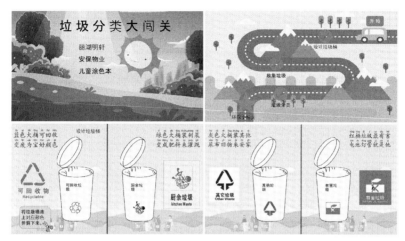

Figure 9.4 Example from the colouring book from the Garbage Sorting project

Figure 9.5 Example of posters from garbage sorting project

environmental project. As previously mentioned, the PDA-designing things form (Table 9.4) is here to assist you in this process. "Materials" refers to whatever you are creating to address the issue you have identified, whether it's posters and videos for a campaign, community activities, or any other project components.

Remember, the materials you design are the final step in the PDA-designing things form. Use the provided questions and the material senses table to guide your development process. These questions will help you consider the importance of your design and ensure your materials align with your project goals.

You may need to conduct additional research as you design your materials. This could involve gathering facts you want to share with your audience or finding new information that wasn't covered during your literature review. In addition, do share your draft material with your stakeholders and get their feedback. You may also want to pilot your material and update it based on the results and feedback received.

Table 9.3 PDA-designing things – Garbage Sorting project

Names: Xinyi Zhang, Chu Yuan, Changyao Fang, Yuelin Feng

Project title: Garbage Sorting in Li Hu Ming Xuan

Goal/outcomes of the project (what do you hope to achieve)? To educate residents of the garbage sorting system in their city so that they sort rubbish correctly

Where will you be carrying out this project? Give details about the context (including people using the materials) Residents of Li Hu Ming Xuan in China and young children in the community language school. Residents mostly speak Cantonese in the area and so the materials will use Cantonese.

Significance of the project (why is it important to do this)? By educating the residents how to sort garbage properly, it will create a clean, sustainable and liveable community

Material/activity development (what will be created)? Posters depicting how to sort properly will be developed for adults, and a colouring book will be developed for children

What things/readings/projects have you analysed in developing your work? What were some key observations? Readings focused on rules and regulations regarding garbage sorting in the city; social marketing theories; previous campaigns promoting garbage sorting elsewhere

Alignment between design and goals (how do you expect to achieve your goals based on what you will do?) The materials make it clear for the residents how to sort garbage in the appropriate bins making it likely that they will sort rubbish in the appropriate bins

What are some of the challenges that you may face in developing and/or implementing your project? It could be hard to find a collaborator that will help. It could also be challenging to receive permission to display the posters in the residential building.

What are some potential negative consequences of the project and how can you avoid/minimise these? It is possible residents might feel blamed or judged which is why it's important to avoid using language can could negatively judge the residents' behaviours.

Which material senses will your thing/project utilise? How?

	Description	What meanings are being projected?
Sight	Written language; image of bin; images of items for each bin; background of nature	Eye catching slogan at the top of the page, with each description explaining what rubbish goes in each bin. The pictures of the items on each bin and the colour of each bin makes it clear in which bin rubbish must be disposed of. The image of nature in the background emphasises the character "beauty" in the slogan thus creating a positive association between correct garbage sorting and the environment
Sound	Nature background	Although there is no direct use of sound, the background of the posters evokes sounds one might here in nature
Smell	Images of food and other waste on bins	The images of the waste items on each bin evokes the smell of these items, thus creating an association between rubbish and the bins they belong to
Touch	Nil	
Taste	Images of food and other waste on bins	This is similar to the images used to evoke the sense of smell, associating certain tastes to specific bins

Action and continuity

The final stage of a CREDIBLE project is the action and continuity phase. This is where we implement our project to address community needs and create positive change. To implement the Garbage Sorting project, the team joined a WeChat group, allowing them to reach and communicate with all residents. Through WeChat, they distributed posters to educate residents about correct garbage disposal. Additionally, one team member, who worked part-time at the community language school, incorporated the garbage sorting colouring book into her lessons. This ensured that all residents, both children and adults, learned how to sort rubbish correctly. Moreover, the colouring book provided children with an opportunity to practice their handwriting and learn Chinese.

The team documented their project in a comprehensive report, detailing their work for each CREDIBLE stage and including all completed forms and designed materials. This documentation phase was crucial, as it enabled the authors of this book to include the project as a model for others. We will outline the documentation stage in Chapter 10.

Table 9.4 Activity 8 – PDA-designing things form

INSERT MATERIAL DESIGN

Names:

Project title:

Goal/outcomes of the project (what do you hope to achieve)?

Where will you be carrying out this project? Give details about the context (including people using the materials)

Significance of the project (why is it important to do this)?

Material/activity development (what will be created)?

What things/readings/projects have you analysed in developing your work? What were some key observations?

Alignment between design and goals (how do you expect to achieve your goals based on what you will do?)

What are some of the challenges that you may face in developing and/or implementing your project?

What are some potential negative consequences of the project and how can you avoid/minimise these?

Which material senses will your thing/project utilise? How? (Complete the table below for each thing you plan to create)

	Description	What meanings are being projected?
Sight		
Sound		
Smell		
Touch		
Taste		

Activity 9

It is now time to implement your environmental project! Before moving forward, ensure that your stakeholders review and approve your material design to secure a positive response from community members. Additionally, collaborate with your team to set a project implementation date or timeline, making sure, if relevant, that it does not clash with other community events. This is to ensure that there are no other events in the community that might overshadow the implementation of your project.

After implementing the project in the community, thorough documentation is essential. This includes completing both PDA forms and an evaluation of the project's implementation. In your evaluation, detail how the project was carried out and how it was received by the community. You can measure the project's impact by conducting interviews with community members and observing changes in behaviour related to the issue. Part IV of the book includes examples of reports documenting CREDIBLE projects.

The format of your documentation will depend on the nature of the project. It could be a comprehensive portfolio, a video, a written report, or another suitable format. This documentation can then be handed over to the community, enabling them to continue implementing and monitoring the project's outcomes. Additionally, this documentation can serve as a valuable resource for other communities facing similar challenges.

10 It's now your turn to do CREDIBLE!

Now that we have practised how to carry out a CREDIBLE project, it's your turn to implement your own! As shown in Figure 10.1, you first start with the conceptualisation stage, where you identify an issue that your community is facing and identify stakeholders or collaborators from the community who can assist with the project. Once you have identified the issue and target community, you can start conducting research. Investigate similar projects to see if they achieved their outcomes. This is important because you can use a successful project you have identified and conduct a broad PDA analysis on its materials (using Table 10.1). This can help you generate ideas for stage three, the material design stage. Use the PDA-designing things form to answer probing questions about your materials and to guide you in determining how to use the five material senses to connect your target community to your materials. The fourth and final stage is the action and continuation stage. In this stage, you implement your project with the help of your collaborators and document your project. Remember that this stage is continuous. Once you implement your project, you must evaluate its outcomes and determine whether you have achieved your project goals.

Use the questions below to help you throughout the stages of your project.

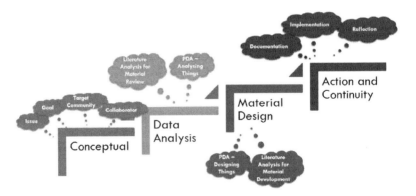

Figure 10.1 Stages of creating a CREDIBLE project

DOI: 10.4324/9781003495086-13

Conceptualisation

- What is the issue/problem you want to address?
- What is the expected impact of this project? Who will benefit from this project and how?
- Who is the target community?
- What is the goal of the project? Is it achievable?
- Who are the relevant stakeholders/collaborators?
- Why do you want to do this project?
- What is the expected timeline of this project?

Data analysis

- What has previously been done to address this issue? Was it in the target community or elsewhere?
- What kind of materials did the projects design? Posters, activities, videos, structure etc.
- Based on your research, were the projects successful in addressing the issues? Why/why not?
- Carry out a PDA analysis of each successful material you would like to learn from Table 10.1.

Table 10.1 PDA-analysing things form template

INSERT MATERIAL

Name the thing:

Describe the thing:

Is this part of a larger campaign/project/program:

If yes, what other materials are part of the campaign? Provide an overview of materials included in the campaign and highlight which things you will analyse. Include a reason for your decision.

What are the goals of the thing?

Context and details about the thing:

- **Who created it?**
- **Why was it created?**

- Where was it created?
- When was it created?

Is there any other necessary information about the material?

Why do you think this thing is successful?

	Description	What meanings are being projected?
Sight		
Sound		
Smell		
Touch		
Taste		

Material design

Use the PDA-designing things form in Table 10.2 to help you with your material design.

Table 10.2 PDA-designing things form template

INSERT MATERIAL DESIGN

Names:

Project title:

Goal/outcomes of the project (what do you hope to achieve)?

Where will you be carrying out this project? Give details about the context (including people using the materials)

Significance of the project (why is it important to do this)?

Material/activity development (what will be created)?

What things/readings/projects have you analysed in developing your work? What were some key observations?

Alignment between design and goals (how do you expect to achieve your goals based on what you will do?

What are some of the challenges that you may face in developing and/or implementing your project?

What are some potential negative consequences of the project and how can you avoid/minimise these?

Which material senses will your thing/project utilise? How? (Complete the table below for each thing you plan to create)

	Description	What meanings are being projected?
Sight		
Sound		
Smell		
Touch		
Taste		

Action and continuity

- Will the community respond positively to the materials/project? Do I need to start with a focus group?
- When is an appropriate time to implement the project? Are there big events happening in the community?
- How do we evaluate the project's success? Is the issue still present in the community? Is it to the same degree as pre-implementation?
- How do we document and handover the project to the community? What is the best format to share what has been done?
- How can we continuously improve the project?

As discussed in previous chapters, a crucial aspect of the CREDIBLE approach is documentation. By documenting our project, we can share our learnings, successes, and areas for improvement with others. One way to document our project is by writing a report and/or giving

Table 10.3 Template for CREDIBLE report

Project title:

Developer name(s):

Author name(s):

Table of contents: Include a table of contents so that the reader can navigate through your report.

Introduction: Introduce your project and provide an outline of what was done, why, and how. Include an outline of the contents of your report.

Material: Share a copy of the material developed (or a link to it).

Establishing CREDIBLITY: Elaborate on how your project is CREDIBLE. To do that, add notes about how your project responds to each letter of the acronym.

    Context:

    Real-world need:

    Engagement and stakeholders:

    Domestic/local knowledge and understandings used (this may include literature and PDA):

    International perspectives (this may include literature and PDA):

    Benefits of the work:

    Lead features of the work:

    Ethical dimensions considered:

Literature review: Briefly outline how you used readings and literature to develop your work. The following workbook provides guidelines on how to write a literature review for project development: www.academia.edu/38944484/How_to_Write_A_Literature_Review_for_Project_Development.

Positive Discourse Analysis: Share your analysis of the successful/good things that you looked at in developing your project. Include information on why this material was good/successful; why were these things relevant to your project; what were some key features of these things; what did they teach you about creating things; how did they help you in developing your own material.

Material development: Describe the material developed. Document how the material was created, its key features, etc. If appropriate, include guidelines and suggestions for others who may want to develop similar material.

> *Implementation*: Describe how/where the material was used. And, if available share some outcomes/evaluation/impact of the work.
>
> *Reflection*: Provide a brief reflection on your project, including suggestions for developing the work further and updating it.
>
> *Appendices*: Include any notes, materials, PDA forms, text/image analyses that are relevant to and support your work. Make sure that you cross-reference all appendices in the body of your report.

presentations. The format of the documentation may vary depending on your audience and method of sharing, but the contents will remain largely consistent. Table 10.3 provides a report template for CREDIBLE project documentation, which can be adapted to different formats as needed.

Part IV

Examples of CREDIBLE projects

Part IV of the book includes four sample CREDIBLE project reports drafted by some of the students enrolled in LNGS7002: Language, Society, and Power, in semester 1 of 2024 at the University of Sydney. Each of the 2500-word (approx.; and not including Appendices) reports looks at a real-world issue observed by the students in their own contexts. The reports document how the students developed their material and the outcomes of their work. These sample reports exemplify both the different issues that can be addressed through a CREDIBLE approach as well as how people can draft their reports for wider dissemination and publication.

To maintain the students' voice, we have limited our editing of their reports. These reports therefore reflect variations in language and stylistic choices but are consistent in terms of organisation and purpose. By recognising and including these language variations, we want to stress that CREDIBLE project reports are about addressing real-word issues and NOT about using standard native-speaker based grammatical choices.

11 Kids Guide to Art in Camden – mapping art spaces and places

Kiyara Grenfell

Introduction

The project "Kids Guide to Art in Camden-Mapping Art Spaces and Places" was developed to make free art spaces in Camden N.S.W. accessible to primary school students, as child visitor numbers are currently very low. This is a problem, as engaging with these spaces is vital to children's wellbeing, education, and development as cultural citizens (Wallis & Noble, 2022). Art museums and galleries "can foster cognitive, aesthetic, kinaesthetic, affective, social, and cultural learning experiences" for young children (Terreni, 2017, p. 14). Likewise, public art constructed with joy and play in mind in open spaces encourages young people's "social, cognitive, verbal, and physical development" (Keyvanfar, Shafaghat, & Rosli, 2022, p. 9). Through my research, two dominant reasons for this lack of engagement emerged: a lack of awareness of these spaces and places, and discomfort with leading children's experiences in the gallery space from teachers and parents. The resource I created as the product of the project aims to tackle these issues. This report will first share a copy of the material developed and demonstrate how it is a CREDIBLE project. Then, it will offer insight into how the project was planned through sharing a literature review and a Positive Discourse Analysis of similar projects. Finally, the report will illustrate how the material was developed, examine its implementation and offer a final reflection.

Material

A copy of the material created for this project can be found in Appendix A. First will be a double-sided A4 colouring-in map of Camden, which aims to familiarise children with Camden art spaces and places. Then, a double-sided A4 activity sheet, to help guide the children's experience in the gallery space to take the pressure off parents and teachers and structure excursions.

DOI: 10.4324/9781003495086-15

Establishing credibility

Context: Child visitor numbers are low in Camden art spaces and places, despite there being a high percentage of children living in the region compared to the rest of NSW (Children and Families, 2024).

Real world need: This is a problem as children report significant benefits by being given access to such spaces.

Engagement and stakeholders: The material is being developed for Camden Council distribution, and as such, feedback from arts and culture administrators has influenced the shape of the project and the Council is likewise funding the printing of the content and supplying the coloured pencils. I've also consulted with local gallery educators, visitor centre employees, parents, kids, and teachers.

Domestic/local knowledge and understandings used: This project uses the knowledge I've picked up as a local, and as someone who works in the Arts and Culture department at Camden Council, and has been developed in collaboration with and for the local community.

International perspectives: The literature I drew from draws upon research and theories that may address international problems but apply to the Camden context regarding guiding children's experiences in galleries.

Benefits of the work: This project is a useful resource for Camden's young people, parents and teachers.

Lead features of the work: The content developed builds upon theories about children's engagement in art spaces. Importantly, it also stands as an example of a CREDIBLE project, contributing to and illustrating the immense benefits of such a way of working.

Ethical dimensions considered: It benefits young students and is offered for free in central locations, making it financially accessible.

Analysis of literature

The project was developed to increase visitor numbers of primary-aged students in art spaces and places in Camden. The literature explored was focused on understanding the problem and considering how the solution could best be developed.

Consultation with local teachers, parents and children uncovered two root causes for the problem. First, there is a general lack of awareness about the existence of these places and spaces. This lack of awareness is partially due to the relatively recent expansion of the art facilities. The Alan Baker Art Gallery was only established in 2018, and the temporary public art exhibitions have been occurring sporadically over the past four years, while much of the public art has only been installed in the past few months. This lack of awareness is also partially due to the distinct lack of information about these places and spaces online and in print. The other factor which is contributing to the low visitor numbers is parent and teacher discomfort with leading experiences in the gallery space. My research found that the discomfort felt in the gallery space by parents and teachers wasn't specific to Camden but rather is a problem faced by institutions globally (Terreni, 2017). It also revealed that statistically, teachers had the most time to be able to take students to gallery spaces through excursions (Terreni, 2017). The materials were developed accordingly. The map was created to raise awareness about the different spaces. The activities would be to guide children through the gallery space, taking the pressure off parents, while also being able to be used by teachers to structure excursions.

The literature consulted gave input as to how the activities could best be developed. It found that if children were to engage in gallery and art spaces, play and hands-on experiences must be integrated with learning (Szeleky, 2014). My research also found that giving students prompts to work out content for themselves significantly increased their ability to retain information (Bridgeman, 2022). As a result, both the map and the activity sheet were developed to encourage children to uncover information for themselves with elements of play. Research consulted also suggested that slow-looking can help students have a deeper understanding of content in gallery spaces, and thus, slow-looking was incorporated into the content through the slow-looking drawing activity (Tate, 2022). Ultimately, the literature drawn upon served to shape the initial project, which was then further tested and developed through feedback.

Positive Discourse Analysis

To help develop my project I looked at three other types of resources: learning resources at the National Gallery of Victoria (NGV), "Burramatta," and existing Camden walking tours and maps.

Learning resources at the NGV: The NGV is an internationally acclaimed art gallery and is known for developing fantastic resources for kids (NGV Kids Activities and Games, 2024). These include booklets with activities where students can create their own versions of works, design their own concepts, and apply their learning. The designs are fun, free, downloadable, and easy to navigate. They often feature the work of artists in the books, and exercises that further students' understanding, encourage slow looking, and allow students to work out ideas for themselves.

These resources served as great inspiration for the activity sheet in particular. Having the sheets as something that could be free, downloadable and printable was inspired by these booklets, as it meant that

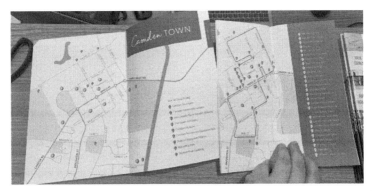

Figure 11.1 Image of existing Camden walking tours and maps, sourced from Camden Visitor Information Centre

teachers would be able to access and print these resources when we send email enquiries.

"Burramatta" (past student project): Early on in the project, Professor Sunny Boy sent me an example of another student's past project. It was a project that mapped a self-guided walk-through Parramatta or "Burramatta", illuminating First Nations knowledge. There were also prompts for activities and exercises along the way.

When developing my own mapping resource I kept this project in mind. I kept the map for the Llewella Davies Memorial Walkway largely blank, with activity prompts so children could fill in the details themselves. I also made sure the map could be taken with parents and children by making it A4 so, like "Burramatta", it could be used as they physically walk through the space.

Existing Camden walking tour and map (Heritage walking tour and map of Camden found in the tourism brochure, from the Camden Visitor Information Centre): The content of this walking tour and map are sparse and offer no activities (Figure 11.1). Instead, they are visual, highlighting only key locations on Camden's main streets.

This influenced the amount of content on my map. My first instinct was to include everything. However, when examining these maps, I noticed that by only focusing on a few key locations the maps ensured these were highlighted. As a result, I stripped back the amount of content I intended to include, and focused on highlighting the key spaces and places, so as to not overwhelm those utilising the resource.

Material development

The project began by first conducting a literature review, applying Positive Discourse Analysis to similar projects, and consulting with local teachers, parents, students, and arts workers. The material

I chose to create from that research was a map that marks out art spaces and places in Camden, and an activity sheet to structure children's visits to the gallery. This content was then further developed in repeated consultation with the listed parties and through testing aspects of its design, all focused on tailoring it to the specific needs of the community.

The original activity sheet was developed by considering how children might best interact with the gallery. Using Adobe InDesign I created a colouring-in of the building and an activity dedicated to slow looking, where children were asked to draw artworks from memory in each room. This was tested at a kids-focused gallery open day, and was offered to the public with free pencils and clipboards (Figures 11.2 and 11.3). I used the findings from the day to further develop the final worksheet: decreasing the size of the sheets to A4 to make them easier to carry around and expanding the activities children found most

Figure 11.2 Table set up from the gallery open day where the activity sheet was tested

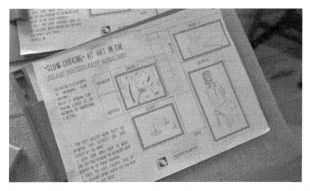

Figure 11.3 Artwork from a child on the gallery open day, utilising the slow looking activity

engaging. I also replaced the colouring-in sheet as it revealed itself to not serve the purpose of guiding experiences in the gallery, with every user of the activity sheet deciding to save it for when they get home. In consultation with arts workers and educators, further changes were made including making the font easier to read and simplifying the text of the written questions and activities (Figure 11.4).

The map was developed by first investigating art spaces and places in Camden through online research, consultation with existing sources, and walking about Camden (Figure 11.5). I made colouring-in components of important places by using Adobe InDesign to trace their dominant outlines. Then, I examined the aerial profile of Camden on Google Maps and determined the space in which they were clustered. I created a not to scale outline of these streets, an outline of Camden's most famous view from John Street for individuals

Figure 11.4 Final feedback notes from arts workers and administrators after final meeting about the activity sheet

Figure 11.5 Public artwork I found at Fergusons Cricket ground from walking around the area, which hadn't been in any of the information about the area online or in print

to orient themselves, and placed the illustrations accordingly. On the page dedicated to the public art trail walk I made it largely blank, with the prompt for children to explore the space for themselves and draw the new artworks installed. I also included written prompts for them to use their senses in this endeavour. In consultation with arts administrators, further changes were also made, including highlighting the senses and simplifying the text.

Implementation

The project's implementation is off to an exciting start. The map will officially be launched at the open day of the public art walkway, now scheduled for the middle of June. After this point, it will be available in the Camden Library, Camden Visitor Information Centre and the Alan Baker Art Gallery. The final activity sheet was made available in the Alan Baker Art Gallery on the 1st of June alongside free pencils and clipboards (Figures 11.6 and 11.7). Over the weekend of the 1st and

Figure 11.6 The set-up of the final activity sheet

Figure 11.7 The gallery room with the activity sheet set-up

2nd, we had a child-focused art workshop within the space. Feedback from the children and parents was incredibly positive, with over half of all those who passed through utilising the resource. Excitingly, the resource resulted in many of the children taking charge of their experience and acting as a guide to their parents. Thus, the resource not only succeeded in taking the pressure off parents to guide gallery experiences but empowered children to be in charge of their learning. Both resources are also being offered as downloadable PDFs to local schools when we send enquiries about school excursions, for teachers to use to facilitate excursions and for students to utilise.

Reflection

This project's development was driven by the specific needs of the Camden community and was tailored to its context through community focused research, exploration, experimentation, testing, and re-evaluation. Its context specific development is its strength. I plan on continuing to develop this work as time passes and incorporate any additional art spaces and places that are built. The activity sheet is intentionally broad to be able to apply to any future exhibitions. However, I also intend on offering editions that work for specific exhibitions, in part to incentivise regular excursions from local schools by emphasising the difference in each. Art can enrich our lives, and yet, so many children are removed from art spaces in Camden. As there is no comparable resource in the region, my hope is it will fill a real need in the community. The colouring-in map raises awareness about these different spaces. The activity sheet empowers parents, teachers and students in the gallery space by giving them the tools to structure their experiences. Hopefully, through their combined use, we will see more kids actively involved and benefiting from their use of Camden's art spaces and places.

References

A guide to slow looking (2022). TATE. Retrieved 1 May 2024, from www.tate.org.uk/art/guide-slow-looking

Bridgeman, A. (2022). *Working it out for themselves: the effect of active learning on student outcomes.* Retrieved 11 September 2022, from https://tinyurl.com/mt3tnut6.

Children and Families (2024). Camden Council. Retrieved 30 April 2024, from www.camden.nsw.gov.au/community/support/children-and-families/

Keyvanfar, A., Shafaghat, A., & Rosli, N.A.L. (2022). A decision support Toolkit for the design of children-oriented urban outdoor learning environments. *Journal of Urban Planning and Development, 148*(3). https://doi.org/10.1061/(ASCE)UP.1943-5444.0000864

NGV Kids Activities and Games (2024). NGV. Retrieved 14 May 2024, from www.ngv.vic.gov.au/kids/ngv-kids-activities/

Szekely, I., & Emilie and Mom Making Art in the Museum. (2014). Creating meaningful art museum experiences for young children: discussions with future art teachers. *Art Education*, 67(4), 34–39. www.jstor.org/stable/24766101

Terreni, L. (2017). Beyond the gates: examining the issues facing early childhood teachers when they visit art museums and galleries with young children in New Zealand. *Australasian Journal of Early Childhood*, 42(3), 14–21. https://doi.org/10.23965/AJEC.42.3.02

Wallis, N., & Noble, K. (2022). Leave only footprints: how children communicate a sense of ownership and belonging in an art gallery. *European Early Childhood Education Research Journal*, 30(3), 344–359. https://doi.org/10.1080/1350293X.2022.2055100

Appendix A

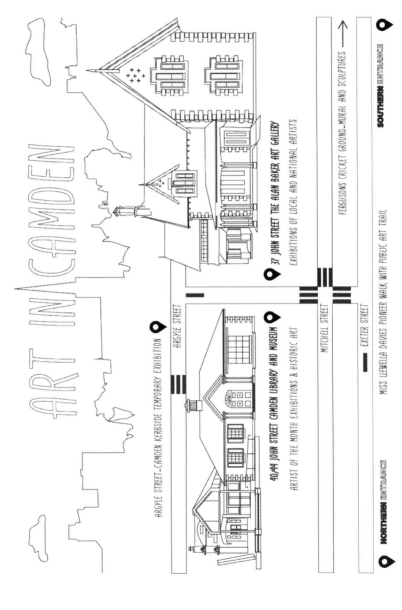

Figure 11.8 Page 1 of a double-sided A4 colouring-in map of Camden

Kids Guide to Art in Camden 133

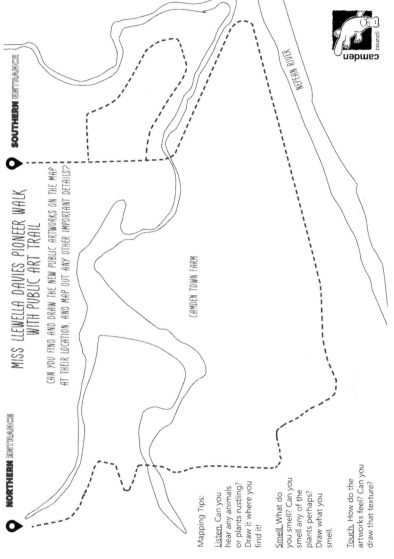

Figure 11.9 Page 2 of a double-sided A4 colouring-in map of Camden

134 Subaltern Linguistics

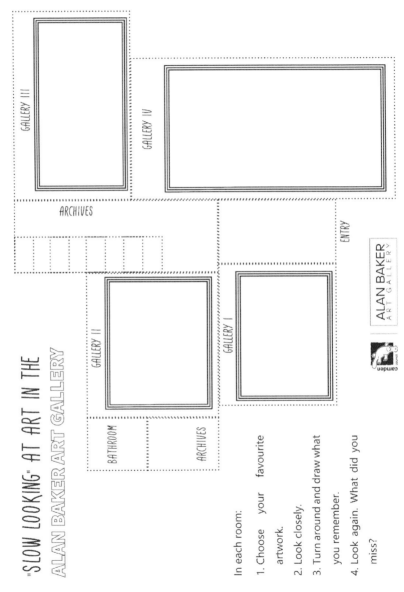

Figure 11.10 Page 1 of a double-sided A4 activity sheet

Kids Guide to Art in Camden 135

Find the information for your favourite painting in the Exhibition Catalogue. Add it in the empty box below.

Artwork title (Date made)
Artist name
Material used, dimensions of work
where the work is from

What emotion do you feel when looking at your favourite painting?

Draw the feeling on the face.

What would the scene sound like?

Would it smell like anything? YES/NO

What would it smell like?

Does it look rough or smooth? YES/NO

What would it feel like?

Why is it your favourite work?

_ _ _ _ _ _ _ _ _ _ _ _ _ _ _ _ _
_ _ _ _ _ _ _ _ _ _ _ _ _ _ _ _ _
_ _ _ _ _ _ _ _ _ _ _ _ _ _ _ _ _
_ _ _ _ _ _ _ _ _ _ _ _ _ _ _ _ _

Does it remind you of anything else?

Figure 11.11 Page 2 of a double-sided A4 activity sheet

12 Cards for Courage

Elisa Ueno, Indiana Salsabila, Qi Wang, and Wenrui Zhang

Introduction

English education in non-English speaking countries may present challenges that can impact students' learning. In the case of China, where English is a mandatory subject in schools, one challenge that can be observed is the tendency for students to be less active in speaking. As half of our groupmates have gone through Chinese education themselves, specifically learning English in China, they have observed that English classes tend to focus more on reading and writing rather than speaking. Due to this disproportionate emphasis on skill sets, speaking is the part in language learning that students tend to find most daunting.

With this project, we aim to combat Chinese students' fear of making mistakes in English class. To facilitate our project, we have contacted a collaborator who is a third-grade English teacher at a Chinese elementary school in Shanghai. Our collaborator informed us that students in English class most commonly make mistakes related to grammar, misreading text, misunderstanding instructions, and organising text. Based on observation, students' fear stems from the possibility of getting mocked by their peers, being the centre of attention, and holding back a group during group work. Based on these findings, we developed a card-based gamification of the narrative genre which will ease students into speaking through collaboration and roleplay. This report will cover the development of our material, from establishing a CREDIBLE approach, reviewing the literature, doing Positive Discourse Analysis (PDA), developing material, implementing, and gathering our reflections.

Material

The material that we have developed can be accessed online via bit.ly/cards-for-courage as well as in Appendix A. These are only the design, as the actual material used is printed.

Establishing credibility

- Context: addresses current circumstance of language education in Chinese elementary school, specifically within a third grade English class;
- Real-world need: supported by testimonials and literature showing that children are fearful of making mistakes in English classes in school;
- Engagement and stakeholders: collaborates with third grade English teacher at Guanlan elementary school in Shanghai, China;
- Domestic/local knowledge and understandings used: material was created using a story from the original textbook that the students are using for their English lesson, and the story is a global folktale acknowledged by locals as a classic childhood story;
- International perspectives: compares ideas with what has already been done to address similar concerns in the field, finding similar trend of gamification of curricula in Chinese English class (e.g. Mr. J's game);
- Benefits of the work: helps the teacher make class more engaging, as well as helping with lesson planning. The material also helps Chinese children with speaking practice and aids in building their confidence with speaking English overall both in and outside of the classroom;
- Lead features of the work: specifically, contributes to foreign language education. In general, contributes to early childhood education;
- Ethical dimensions considered: benefits the local community in the field (both students and teachers). Additionally, the material is not intrusive to the curricula and teaching plan, as the material was built off of the textbook that is currently being used.

Analysis of literature

In a tribute to Hasan, Mahboob (2015) introduces a possible reason as to why students perform differently in school; the ability to read through resemanticisation. According to Hasan, resemanticisation is the manipulation of word meaning, often using language of "affective colouring" to disguise what is really being said. Therefore, students who can read through resemanticisation can understand what is truly being said and thus have an advantage over students who cannot. Hasan theorises that there are different types of literacy and that reflection literacy is necessary to read through resemanticisation. However,

Hasan indicates that reflection literacy is not taught in schools. The only place in which a student can learn this is if they are raised in an environment in which it is naturally taught. Therefore, depending on the environment in which they are raised, students perform differently in school.

Similar to how Mahboob (2015) underlines the importance of prior knowledge, Rose (2014) also considers commonsense knowledge as an important key that can ensure participation in learning. By analysing classroom learning as a pedagogic discourse with genre and register theory, he highlights how the curriculum genre encompasses dialogic discourse which opens the possibility of negotiating knowledge. The analysis explores exchange structures, learning cycles, and multimodal sources of meanings that could provide a framework for teaching evaluation. In the context of this project, the findings from this paper help highlight the importance of an equal starting point among students when carrying out pedagogic activity, especially in the early phases of the learning cycle. It also provides a basis for teaching evaluation to create inclusive learning where all students can participate equally.

Drawing from the insights of Permana et al. (2023), which underscore the positive impact of gamification in language learning through tools like Quizizz, our card game aims to leverage these benefits by creating a playful and engaging environment that fosters English language practice among Chinese third graders. Similarly, Martin and Matthiessen (2014) highlight the critical roles of modelling and mentoring in language acquisition, principles our game integrates by allowing students to learn from peer interactions within structured gameplay, thereby reducing the fear of making mistakes and enhancing their linguistic confidence.

To be more convincing, we discovered three different Chinese blogs that analyse parents' psychological and behavioural dimensions based on real experiences from Chinese teachers. The blogs address students' fear of making mistakes in class by providing answers through three approaches: What, Why, and How. Investigating the relationship between children's fear and parents' attitudes, the blog uses the example of an elementary school child who shifted from confident to frightened and sensitive in the face of academic and social expectations to argue that there are two types of parental mindsets: growth mindset and fixed mindset. The fixed mindset can have psychological effects on children, such as becoming responsibility-shy and lacking the courage and motivation to explore and develop new skills or interests, making it difficult for them to cope with life's challenges and adversities and eventually lowering their self-confidence and self-esteem. Secondly, how this fear formed is analysed. According to the blogs, the reason for this is that parents continually and impatiently point out their children's faults, which not only demonstrates that parents lack confidence in their children, but also makes the youngsters believe that they are continuously incorrect and thus develop fear of being wrong. Measures taken to address this issue include giving praise for students' "effort" rather than "talent" in their daily lives, teaching students to look positively at mistakes, and fostering a "growth mindset" atmosphere.

In addition to the written literature, we also had extended conversations with the teachers in the school. An example of one of these exchanges is shared in Appendix B.

Positive Discourse Analysis

To develop the right materials, two teaching resources were analysed through Positive Discourse Analysis (PDA). The full PDA can be found in Appendix C.

a. Kings Game (Mr. J China ESL)

   The Kings Game, as detailed in Appendix C, was thoroughly analysed using Positive Discourse Analysis (PDA) to understand its educational efficacy and inclusivity in language teaching. This game uniquely facilitates active learning by allowing students to assume leadership roles, thus fostering a sense of responsibility and enhancing communication skills. Through its interactive and engaging format, the Kings Game encourages students to practice English in a supportive group setting, promoting both linguistic skills and social interaction. The use of direct commands and questions in the game mechanics supports the development of practical language usage, mirroring real-life scenarios. This game, developed by experienced ESL instructors, is particularly effective in reducing classroom anxiety and encouraging spontaneous language use, making it a valuable resource for language acquisition in diverse educational settings.

b. Card Game: Story-Builder (SCOLAR)

   Sponsored by the Standing Committee on Language Education and Research (SCOLAR) Hong Kong, Teacup Productions (HK) Limited developed a storytelling kit for a competition targeted at primary school students in Hong Kong, which includes a card game. This game creatively addresses Chinese students' fear of speaking in a foreign language by using gamification based on the narrative genre. Beyond introducing narrative structure, the kit includes a dice with illustrations of emotions which allows students to be more comfortable with expressive speaking. The project, which includes not only English but also Mandarin and the local language Putonghua, does not only develop students' confidence in public speaking, but also enhances their multilingual comprehension and articulation skills. It also takes language learning beyond conventional reading and writing, as the activity involves roleplay that engages the human senses, notably sight, sound, and touch.

Material development

Initially, we were planning to make a storybook that could help address students' fear of making mistakes in class. However, we found that there were limitations to resources such as publishers and illustrators, as well as time constraints.

In consideration of our target beneficiaries who are young learners, we tried to reconfigure our material into something simpler yet still able to encourage engagement and active participation in class. In the early stages of our project ideation, we considered a card game that involved pulling vocabulary words and creating a story out of them. However, we found that creating a story from zero could incite anxiety amongst young students, hence worsening their fear of making mistakes. Therefore, we looked into the existing teaching material that our collaborator provided and found the Three Little Pigs, a story that is already popular among young audiences in China. As the textbook featured only dialogues, we needed to make sure that our material included narrative sentences. We then explored and compared different narrative versions of the original story to write the sentences, consulting our collaborator to ensure they were appropriate for the students' proficiency level.

The current version of our card deck has two different sides, with one side having the narrative sentences and the other side having the dialogue with illustrations from the textbook. We designed the material this way in order to facilitate the two main activities involving roleplay and arranging narrative sequences. In consideration of the learning cycle, we realised that our material must ensure that all students started with a similar or equal commonsense to encourage participation. Therefore, other than having an equal start from the same deck of cards, the students will also have the same level of knowledge about the story as the teacher will recite it prior to the game.

From our preliminary survey with the collaborator, we found that students would be more scared when they have to work in big groups. This is why our activity puts students into pairs to arrange the cards in the correct order first. Gradually easing the students into teamwork, paired students will then form a four-person group to act out the complete story to the class. To conclude the activity, the teacher will correct students' mistakes while emphasising that despite errors, students can still understand each other at the end of the class.

After going through the process of developing our material, we have identified the strengths and weaknesses that could provide guidance for similar future projects. We suggest that, given more opportunity to access resources, developer(s) should involve more collaborators such as an illustrator to make the material more visually engaging and facilitate tailored narratives beyond the textbook version. It will also be ideal to use stories that students are already familiar with, such as popular folktales or existing stories in the school curricula. Beyond the card deck material, we also have suggestions for the implementation: it is important to ensure that the class activity does not involve big groups from the start, so that students are allowed to ease out of their fear gradually throughout the learning process. Finally, it is essential to have the teacher highlight that despite making mistakes, students can still understand each other and even see errors as part of the learning process.

Implementation

This card game will be implemented in a third grade English class in a Chinese elementary school. To ensure that this project does not interfere with the existing teaching schedule and curriculum, we have agreed with the collaborator to implement it in the upcoming month when the syllabus reaches the Three Little Pigs module. However, we have done a try-out as well as discussed with the collaborator to evaluate the effectiveness of this material.

From a try-out of the activity with a young learner, as documented in Appendix D, we found that the material was effective in lessening fear of making mistakes mostly due to the story's familiarity. The activity could also foster a supportive environment where learners feel comfortable and confident in expressing themselves because they engage with a familiar story and interact with familiar people (peers and/or teacher). However, the visuals on the card could be bigger, hence not only depending on the textbook but potentially original illustrations. In addition, children could occasionally be distracted from the activity, meaning that the cards or overall activity may need more elements that can ensure better immersion.

From the collaborator's perspective, the game could potentially address students' fear of holding the group back, because they will be working neither alone nor in a big group at the first stage of the activity. The collaborative stage of the activity eases the students from pairs to a four-person group, allowing students time to build more confidence and comfort. In addition, this material could also help lessen the fear of making grammatical errors, because students will focus more on the storytelling and performance aspects rather than making possible mistakes, especially as the collaborator highlighted that only teachers notice the faults made by students. Furthermore, the cards will provide assistance and boost students' sense of security when performing in case they forget the lines of the story. As a final point, this card game is designed to be implemented through several steps which gradually eases students' fear of making mistakes in class. At the same time, the roleplay can help evoke students' interest and open room for them to be active.

Reflection

Originally, our group had started off with the idea of addressing the fear of making mistakes in a math class within Chinese elementary schools, as math always has a fixed answer which clearly determines students as either right or wrong. However, after consulting with Professor Mahboob, our focus shifted towards Chinese students in an English class. This is because none of us were math experts, but all of us had experience in learning English and taking English classes. Furthermore, we had two group members who had lived the realities of learning English in Chinese schools. This new direction allowed us to draw on our knowledge and experiences, letting us provide interdisciplinary and cross-cultural perspectives in developing the material.

These weeks of iterating our prototype were valuable to our group, as it forced us to think critically about the *why* every step of the way. We learned that language can reflect power dynamics within educational settings (students performing differently factorised by communication used in learning at home and school) and understood the importance of being informed by lived realities to create an effective learning material.

In the future, it may be beneficial to improve our material by printing the material as laminated cards. We could also explore making card decks of different children's stories and potentially collaborating with ESL educators in other countries.

References

Mahboob, A. (2015). Language, literacy, education, and empowerment: a tribute to Ruqaiya Hasan. *Journal of World Languages*, 2(2–3), 144–155. https://doi.org/10.1080/21698252.2016.1191140

Martin, J., & Matthiessen, C. (2014). Modelling and Mentoring: Teaching and Learning from Home Through School. In: A. Mahboob & L. Barratt. (Eds.), *Englishes in Multilingual Contexts. Multilingual Education*, vol 10 (pp. 137–163). Springer. https://doi.org/10.1007/978-94-017-8869-4_9

Mr. J China ESL. (n.d.) *Kings.* www.mrjchinaesl.com/kings.html

Permana, P., Permatawati, I., & Khoerudin, E. (2023). Foreign language learning gamification using Quizizz: a systematic review based on students' perception. *Eralingua*, 7(2), 233–249. https://doi.org/10.26858/eralingua.v7i2.23969

Rose, D. (2014). Analysing pedagogic discourse: an approach from genre and register. *Functional Linguistics*, 1(11), 1–32. https://doi.org/10.1186/s40554-014-0011-4

SCOLAR. (2022). *The Art of Storytelling Booklet*. https://scolarhk.edb.hkedcity.net/sites/default/files/media/TAT%2022-23%20The%20Art%20of%20Storytelling%20Booklet.pdf

昭德心理. (2022, April 18). 孩子玻璃心、害怕犯错，与你的这种思维方式有关……. C.m.163.com. https://c.m.163.com/news/a/H58DDMUE0542TCCT.html

网易. (2024, January 23). "害怕犯错"的心理是怎样形成的？www.163.com. www.163.com/dy/article/IP5DMAB50517A5LR.html

周木木. (2020, March 7). 孩子害怕犯错、遇事不敢挑战？"成长型思维"帮孩子重新认识自己. Toutiao.com. www.toutiao.com/article/6801029286758187523/

Appendix A

Figure 12.1 Images of cards created for the project – sheet 1

144   Subaltern Linguistics

Figure 12.2 Images of cards created for the project – sheet 2

Figure 12.3 Images of cards created for the project – sheet 3

Figure 12.4 Images of cards created for the project – sheet 4

Appendix B

Questionnaire about children's performance in school with the collaborator

(Background: Urban school, Grade 3, English class)

Q: What kind of mistakes do students usually make in the English class?

A: Students often make grammar mistakes, misread words in paragraphs, or cannot understand the teacher's instructions. For example, when the teacher asks in class, 'Do you like pandas?' She expects the students to answer the question, but students often understand it as requiring them to repeat after the teacher.

Q: Why do you think students are afraid of making mistakes in class?

A: The first point is that if they answer incorrectly, their classmates around them will mock them; the second point is that they fear being the centre of attention; the third point is that during group work if other group members are more capable, the weaker students will be worried about holding the group back.

Q: What are the typical reactions of students after making a mistake?

A: The first behaviour is that, after answering a question incorrectly, even if the teacher asks simpler questions afterward, they are unable to respond. The second is a loss of confidence, resulting in decreased participation in class.

Q: What are the common traits among capable classmates?

A: Most of them have a solid understanding of their subjects and serve as role models for their classmates in daily studies. They often receive praise from teachers as well.

(P.S.: However, once these students make even the slightest mistake or receive criticism from teachers or parents, they experience a psychological breakdown and are unwilling to face their parents or teachers.

We speculate that this is because they face excessive expectations, not only from teachers and parents but also from their peers.)

Q: Do you think having different accents is an issue in English classes today?

A: No. It's very common but we still try to guide their accents to be more in line with the textbook tapes.

(P.S.: Today, parents have higher levels of education compared to before, enabling them to teach their children English after school. However, parents also encounter difficulties in reading words correctly. Therefore, we still advocate that during primary school, it's better for children to follow along with the teacher's reading in class and practice listening to tapes on their own after class).

Appendix C

Complete PDA analysis of two similar projects

Teaching resource 1:

Name: Card Game: Kings

Description: Designed by Mr. J (Matt Johanson), this game is an interactive classroom activity where students role-play as kings, issuing commands in English to their peers, thus enhancing their language skills through leadership roles, immediate application of vocabulary, and promoting confident communication in a fun, engaging setting.

Goals: To assist the teaching process as well as help build their language skills in a practical, memorable and enjoyable way.

Context and details

Who created it: Mr. J (Matt Johanson)

When was it created: 2018

Other info: Online resource available for free

Reference: www.mrjchinaesl.com/kings.html

Why was it successful: The Kings Game proved successful primarily due to its immersive and interactive approach, which significantly enhances student engagement and participation in language learning. By placing students in the role of "kings" who must use English to give commands to their peers, the game transforms the classroom into a dynamic environment where language learning becomes a part of active play rather than passive study. This role-playing element not only makes learning more enjoyable but also helps students practice language skills in a context that simulates real-life interactions.

Table 12.1

	Description	Meanings projected
Sight	Students observe each other performing actions and speaking commands using colourful props or cards.	Visual cues foster engagement and indicate the game's interactive nature, encouraging active participation and attentiveness.
Sound	The classroom is filled with the sounds of students issuing commands and responding to each other in English.	Auditory stimulation through active dialogue and response promotes language fluency and auditory learning, suggesting a dynamic learning environment.
Smell	-	-
Touch	Students physically handle game materials such as cards and possibly move around the room as part of the game dynamics.	Tactile interactions with game components and movement in the space emphasise kinaesthetic learning, enhancing memory and engagement through physical activity.
Taste	-	-

Teaching resource 2:

Name: Card Game: Story Builder

Description: A storytelling kit developed by Teacup Productions (HK) Limited, sponsored by Standing Committee on Education Language and Research (SCOLAR), to help Chinese primary school students with public speaking in their non-native language and language learning in general.

Part of campaign: It is part of a three-tiered competition called "Tell A Tale: Children's Storytelling Competition" that focuses on storytelling with different types of teaching resources.

Goals: To address students' fear of speaking in foreign languages

Context and details

Who created it: Teacup Productions (HK) Limited, sponsored by SCOLAR

When was it created: 2022

Other info: Online resource available for free

Reference: https://scolarhk.edb.hkedcity.net/sites/default/files/media/TAT%2022-23%20Storywriting%20kit.pdf

Why was it successful: Beyond introducing narrative structure, the kit also includes a dice with illustrations of emotions which allows students to be invested emotionally in the storyline. The project, which includes not only English but also a local language (Putonghua), is formatted as a competition which opens equal opportunity for all students. This means that the game will not only develop students' confidence in public speaking, but also enhance their comprehension and articulation skills in English and Chinese (including Putonghua). It also takes language learning beyond conventional reading and writing, as the activity involves a roleplay.

Table 12.2

	Description	**Meanings projected**
Sight	Cards with images illustrating different narratives	The illustrations provide concrete visualisation of the narratives, aiding students with meaning making and manifesting their ideas from the story
	Dice with a panda illustration on each side representing different emotions	The panda's facial expressions help students make connection between the English words and the range of emotions
Sound	Texts of narrative in three languages	When recited, students can hear how the same story is delivered in different languages
	Speech bubble and sound effect text in illustration	Evokes dialogues and sounds involved in the story
Smell	-	-
Touch	Card deck	Touching the card deck physically and arranging them in order allows students to see narrative structure in a more tangible way
	Emotion dice	Rolling the dice gives a dynamic element to the learning process and a sense of power over the emotions needed for the roleplay
Taste	-	-

Appendix D

Card game try-out and feedback

1. Did participating in the activity help students feel more comfortable expressing themselves in English? **Yes / No**
   Comment: The media is great because kids are familiar with the 3 Little Pigs story, however the picture might be too small as kids used to playing with flashcards with bigger pictures.

Cards for Courage   149

Figure 12.5 A child playing with the cards created during the pilot study

Figure 12.6 A child playing with the cards created during the pilot study

2. How did the students feel about making mistakes during the activity? (You may ask the students)
   Very afraid
   Somewhat afraid
   Not too afraid
   Not afraid at all
   Comment: They're not afraid at all because the game itself is a fun activity they do with people who they are comfortable with and they like the 3 Little Pigs story.

3. How has the activity impacted students' understanding of the importance of making mistakes in the learning process?
   Reinforced the belief that mistakes are bad
   Made them realise mistakes are essential for learning
   ***Comment:* Didn't change any perspective**

4. On a scale of 1 to 5, how confident do the students seem to be now about speaking up during the learning process?
   1: Not confident at all
   2: Slightly confident
   3: Moderately confident
   4: Very confident
   5: Extremely confident

5. What aspect of the activity seemed to be the most helpful in overcoming students' fear of making mistakes?
   Comment: **Storytelling with familiar stories.**

6. Did the activity engage the students from start to finish? If not, what factor could play in making the students not participate?
   Comment: **Not all the time, as kids are easily distracted by other toys/activities.**

13 Gender stereotypes in fairy tales: the CREDIBLE Project's journey of designing a workshop

Syeda Sughra Naqvi, Jingchen Shi, Xinyan Wang, and Yue Shu

Introduction

Gender stereotypes present in fairy tales serve as a mirror reflecting societal norms and beliefs, often reinforcing detrimental notions about the expected roles and behaviours of both men and women. Particularly in regions like Pakistan, where gender bias is deeply ingrained, these stereotypes wield significant influence on individuals' self-perception and the perceptions of others. Women, frequently marginalised and deprived of educational opportunities, unintentionally uphold these stereotypes by adhering to traditional gender norms. To combat this pervasive issue, a holistic approach called CREDIBLE is implemented. This approach involves Contextually relevant material, Responding to the issue, Engaging local collaborators, and incorporating Domestic understandings while integrating International knowledge through Positive Discourse Analysis (PDA) for the betterment of society. At the forefront of this initiative is a newly devised workshop aimed at deconstructing and challenging gender stereotypes embedded in classic fairy tales like *Aladdin*, *Snow White*, and *Sleeping Beauty*. Fairy tales hold significance as they mirror societal and cultural values (Sharif, 2016). The workshop meticulously examines both the original and modern interpretations of these tales to unveil the ingrained gender biases. It scrutinises the undue focus on female characters' physical appearances, the portrayal of women as passive individuals in need of rescue, and the lack of diversity in female representation. Through interactive exercises and discussions, participants are urged to critically evaluate these stereotypes and contemplate alternative narratives. By viewing videos, analysing various renditions of *Aladdin*, dissecting clips from *Snow White*, and exploring the historical context of these tales, participants will develop a deeper comprehension of how gender

DOI: 10.4324/9781003495086-17

stereotypes are formulated and perpetuated. Moreover, through engaging in creative storytelling activities, participants are afforded the opportunity to challenge prevailing stereotypes and craft more varied and empowering narratives. The overarching objective of this endeavour is to empower community members to interpret fairy tales through a contemporary, inclusive perspective, fostering critical thinking and raising awareness about gender stereotypes in literature and society. By catalysing a shift towards progressive and egalitarian viewpoints, the CREDIBLE project endeavours to confront and dismantle entrenched gender stereotypes, paving the way for a fairer and more just society.

Establishing credibility

We worked on this project following the CREDIBLE approach and to establish that the project is CREDIBLE, we are to consider all its dimensions that include:

i) Contextual Relevance: gender stereotypes in fairy tales are associated with how these narratives shape the perceptions of gender roles in society, especially among young generations. The project aims not only to make the young generation aware of stereotypes but also to encourage them to make changes regarding this issue;

ii) Responds to Practical Needs: United Nation Development Programme Report (UNDP, 2022–2023) pointed out, "Pakistan ranks 145th out of 146 countries on the World Economic Forum's 2022 Global Gender Gap Index, and 161st out of 191 countries on the Human Development Report's 2022 Gender Inequality Index. There is an urgent need to closely examine the factors contributing to this state of gender in Pakistan". That is, Pakistani women are subjected to structural barriers that deny them their fundamental rights, including the ability to inherit property, pursue education and their careers, and confront gender bias in the workplace. These hinder women's empowerment, which results in their financial dependence on males. Hence, this project helps spreading awareness and empowering the subaltern voices Pakistani society is in dire need of;

iii) Engagement of the Local Community: we engaged the local community by contacting the folk educationists and students for this subaltern practice. They have already managed to conduct the pilot on 29th May 2024 and will also be involved in the final dissemination of the project in July. Many other stakeholders from different cities; educationists, private NGOs, social welfare workers, and so on have shown their interest to collaborate for this awareness drive;

iv) Domestic Familiarity: the domestic understanding is derived through the literature and scholarly works presented by the local writers and scholars. The details are shared in the Literature Review and PDA section;

v) International Representations: we also consulted the recognised global perspectives addressing gender stereotypes in fairy tales to achieve the goal of the project;

vi) Benefits Expected: this project aims to not only spread awareness but also stimulate the thinking process questioning gender stereotypes prevalent in the society. The process may be slower (pilot study indicates) but in the long run, we expect better results and a change that helps evolve a more inclusive society;

vii) Lead in Feature: designing a workshop. To achieve the CREDIBLE project's endeavours, we designed a workshop that will help spread a better understanding of the gender stereotypes as well as will provoke the audience to work for a change in society;

viii) Ethically Informed Project: we considered all the ethical dimensions practiced worldwide as well as in Asian societies. Inclusive equity and equality towards genders is an urgent requirement of the social values and norms for a better social representation and status for all.

Material developed

- Slides (with videos) used in the workshop:
  https://tinyurl.com/mwrvmfhj
- Instruction for collaborators:
  https://docs.google.com/document/d/1w3jw60h3y-jn68xJTmjG PHDMVluPw1NT5wXalgJx_78/edit?usp=sharing
- Handout for participants: Please see Appendix 2.

Analysis of literature

Sharif (2016) justified why fairy tales are salient regarding gender stereotypes. Sharif (2016) explored the evolution of gender roles and stereotypes in fairy tales from the original version to Disney retelling versions. She claimed that fairy tales always reflect the cultural and social values that cater to the domination of patriarchal society. Thus, the presentation of stereotyped gender images would influence the perceptions and expectations of females in the society. Jimenez (2022) also pointed out that the biased representation of Disney female characters negatively affects women from multiple perspectives. Therefore, from the written word to the big screen, the portrayal of gender in fairy tales has recorded the gender inequality suffered by women; on the other hand, deconstructing the gender stereotypes in fairy tales can effectively make society reflect on and change the gender issue. As Meland (2020) found, a fairy tale is not merely a tale rather it is a flexible carrier to challenge the stereotypes.

What are the gender stereotypes in fairy tales

Cekiso (2013) found that gender stereotypes in selected IsiXhosa and English fairy tales involve the promotion of physical beauty ideals and the consistent portrayal of female characters as weak and dependent. Veselá (2014) explored the presence of gender roles, stereotypes, and biases in fairy tales by analysing the portrayal of Cinderella and Snow White, and concluded that "women are those who are frequently depicted in an inferior and passive role in the fairy tales" (p. 56). Sharif (2016) also claimed that the male characters in fairy tales are always "more active and independent" (p. 51) than female characters. In addition, Sharif (2016) noticed that the female characters who have the masculine features (e.g., ambition and power) would be depicted as evil, suggesting that women are not supposed to own ambition and power. Jimenez (2022) offered a more detailed analysis of Disney animated versions of fairy tales. She analysed that, while the animated version of *Aladdin* tried to construct gender-neutral plots, the portrayals of female characters remained biased (e.g., Jasmine was sexualised to cater to the male gaze; the underrepresentation of women; a traditional happy ending). Overall, these readings greatly contribute to the presentation content in the workshop.

The theoretical framework

As mentioned before, the project aims not only to make the young generation aware of stereotypes but also to encourage them to make changes regarding this issue. Social cognitive theory enables participants in the workshop to make changes regarding gender stereotypes. Social cognitive theory posits that humans will be influenced by the environment and thus change their behaviours; also, humans will influence the environment through changing their behaviours. That is, person, behaviour and environment construct a triangle, in which the three elements are reciprocally interacting (Bandura, 1988). Thus, the workshop will construct a social context, in which the participant will change their cognition of gender stereotypes through a series of activities, and then change their behaviours in reality.

Methodology

We will conduct workshops in Pakistan with the active participation of our collaborators. We developed a five-stage structure that includes lead-in, presentation, practice, production, and wrap-up. This is adapted from Situational Language Teaching (SLT) phases: "Presentation", "Practice", "Production" (PPP). The PPP method posits acquisition entails initially receiving new information, subsequently consolidating it in memory, and ultimately employing it in practical application until becoming habitual (Frisby, 1957, p. 136; as cited in Lennon, 2021). This is consistent with our goals.

We plan to first present the frequent gender stereotypes in *Aladdin* to make participants realise; then, practise by asking them to find gender stereotypes in *Snow White* and discuss the factors and impacts; then finally, through discussing *Maleficent* to encourage them to alter the stereotypes. During the process, we employ a methodology that enables our collaborators and youth participants to identify and challenge gender stereotypes. With multimodal materials as the primary means of conveying meaning, the workshop is centred on youth participants who will be made aware of and challenge gender stereotypes in fairy tales through various activities, and the collaborators are facilitators who, while guiding the workshop, are also identifying and challenging stereotypes.

Positive Discourse Analysis

An academic video: https://youtu.be/emwvWqQ0JQI?si=ko8s3sJ3kkixRYyp

Cheung's (2011) academic video *Racial and gender ideologies in 4 Disney/Pixar featured animations: Cars, Ratatouille, WALL-E and UP*, published on YouTube, was part of her project for the unit Language, Society, and Power in the Department of Linguistics in the University of Sydney in Semester 1, 2011. It analyses the underlying social ideologies in four Disney/Pixar animations. One of the arguments (i.e., female social status) is related to our gender stereotypes workshop. This video clearly breaks down the analysis into four parts according to the arguments and combines it with the clips from animations. In addition, this video critically analyses the animations from an academic perspective balanced with plain and short sentences to fit the dynamic and engaging mode of the video. Furthermore, the video proposes a rhetorical question at the end to involve the participants. Overall, this video compellingly combines visual elements, interactive mode, and academic analysis to reveal how the mainstream animated film reflects ideas on racial and gender issues. We adapted this model to structure our engaging and informative videos. However, we shortened the length of the videos to prioritise allocating more time for participants to respond to and engage in interactive activities in person.

A flyer: www.bodysafetyaustralia.com.au/images/PDFs/Final-Flyer-GG-PD.pdf (a copy of the flyer can be found in Appendix 5)

The flyer is for the Gender equity and inclusion Professional Development workshop. This workshop aims to train "staff from early learning to Year 12 exploring creating inclusive and equitable environments for boys, girls and gender non-conforming children". This flyer successfully employs multimodal texts, that is, written and visual texts work together to convey the meaning. It employs the power of colour to strengthen the positive affection of the audience and deliver the message. For example, the use of green is consistent with the meaning of "safety" (see Figure 13.1). In addition, the rainbow symbolises the LGBTQIA+ topic in the workshop (see Figure 13.2). Also, the flyer uses different styles and bold to highlight the keywords in a long paragraph (see Figure 13.3), which is conducive to attracting the audience's attention to salient information. These features initially inspired us to create a poster for our workshop; later, as we did not need to promote our workshop, we adapted it to produce our handout instead. However, since the flyer is for promotional purposes while the handout is for pedagogical, the design accordingly changed. For example, written text in the flyer aligned to the centre while the handout aligned the left to cater to the writing path from the left to the right. In addition, the layout of the whole flyer was a centre-margin arrangement to emphasise the detailed information in the middle, while the handout followed the reading path to arrange the content in order from top to bottom.

A YouTube video course: www.youtube.com/watch?v=j0wv-qZ2toI

Alvira's (2020) video discusses Gender Stereotypes, which is closely related to our topic. It logically structures the content with four parts: what is gender stereotype, how to identify gender stereotypes,

Figure 13.1 An example of how format and style are used to add to meaning of the text

Figure 13.2 An example of the use of format and style to symbolise the LGBTQIA+ topic

Our Gender Glorious program is a **gender equity and inclusivity** professional learning workshop for staff from early learning to Year 12 exploring creating **inclusive and equitable environments** for boys, girls and gender non-conforming children. Offered as either **one full day, one half day or one 2 hour session**, our gender equity and inclusion Professional Development supports your **Child Safe Standards, Respectful Relationships curriculum** and covers the following:

Figure 13.3 An example of use of different font and style features to highlight keywords

impact of gender stereotypes, dealing with gender stereotypes. This video effectively provided a pedagogical sequence for presenting the knowledge in our workshop; thus, we adapted the sequences to draft our workshop. First, participants will be informed what gender stereotype is; next, they will be prepared with frequent gender stereotypes in fairy tales; then, they will explore the factors and impacts of gender stereotypes; finally, they will engage in retelling discussions to challenge gender stereotypes.

Material development

Material development is an ever-changing process. It started with an identification of target audience and goals. The project, through a workshop, aimed to raise the youth participants' awareness of gender stereotypes through fairy tales and challenge them. Accordingly, the materials aimed to guide participants to recognise them and to make alternative narratives. The materials were created to be multimedia, incorporating various elements such as slides, videos, handouts, and instructions to better engage collaborators and young participants. More importantly, the content is improved after the pilot workshop to be more effective in the formal workshop.

Timeline

Table 13.1 Timeline for the project

Week 4	• Formed a team
Week 5	• Proposed/discussed ideas
Week 6	• Initial idea: fairy tales rewriting
	• Planned to design a workshop
Week 7	• Literature Review
	• PDA
Week 8	• Finalised the content: Aladdin; Snow White; Sleeping Beauty (Maleficent)
Week 9	• Designed framework & structure of the workshop: The Product
Week 10	• Drafted the materials
Week 11	• Transformed the materials into a final product: The Workshop
	• Scheduled pilot
Week 12	• Presented the materials to the class

Slides and video

The slides are the visualisation of the workshop stages. They were created with a templet in Canva, an online design and visual communication platform. The core elements in the slides, even in the workshop, are the videos. It facilitates active participation throughout the workshop.

Lead-in employed a clip from Ralph Breaks the Internet to activate the schema of stereotyped princess. This clip was extracted from a YouTube video published by Disney UK (2018, Nov 21).

Presentation applied videos created by Jingchen Shi with iMovie, a video editor (www.apple.com/au/imovie/). They were employed to present the stereotypes in three different versions of *Aladdin* respectively.

Practice included a video created by Xinyan Wang with CapCut, a video editor (www.capcut.com). It was employed to help participants practice identifying the gender stereotypes in *Snow White* and then analysing the factors and impacts.

Production featured a video created by Yue Shu with iMovie. It was employed to discuss the retold version of *Sleeping Beauty*, that is *Maleficent*, and thus encourage participants to retell the ending of *Snow White* in the last discussion activities.

Note: See Appendix1 for the detailed content development of the selected fairy tales.

Handout for participants

The handout (see Appendix 2) was drafted by Jingchen Shi with Microsoft PowerPoint, then, Syeda Sughra Naqvi, Xinyan Wang, and Yue Shu gave the final confirmation. It was structured in a way that guides participants through various activities, functioning as an outline of the workshop. Notably, the handout was not required to fill all the blanks, since the prominent activities were discussions to engage participants rather than writings. The handouts are mainly used to take notes.

Instruction for collaborators

The instruction was created to guide collaborators on how to facilitate the workshop. It was in accordance with the slides, thus there were cross-references between the slides and the instruction.

Implementation

The collected material has been transformed into designing a workshop. The newly designed workshop/s will be conducted in Pakistan, Australia and China. The workshop has already been conducted as a pilot practice in Pakistan by our collaborators who are working in the Higher Education Department of Punjab, Pakistan. Shaista Afzaal, an Assistant Professor of English currently posted at the Government Graduate College for Women Sahiwal, conducted the Workshop on 29th May 2024 while Prof. Sumera Nasim, an Associate Professor of English and the Principal of the Government Graduate College for Women Farid Town, Sahiwal facilitated her by providing all the requirements to hold it. The participants were the 8th semester students of the BS 4 Years Program in the Discipline of English of the same College. The age range of the participants, as planned, was from 18 to 24 years. The feedback on the handouts and group discussions is annexed as Appendix 3 and photos and video clips of the pilot as Appendix 4. The collaborators also shared their views about the workshop.

For example, Sumera Nasim, the organiser of the pilot workshop in Pakistan said: "It is a *pakki pakaai kheer* (ready to serve) for us. No particular effort was required except profound reading as everything is elaborated through instructions very comprehensively. The students found the activities exciting. Fairy tales always provide an escape and shelter to the girls in the type of society we live in. So, the response was typical. The students were more interested in the character of the prince than the princess. However, during the activities, their discussion and written expression reflected a slightly different yet thought-provoking perspective that may be strengthened with the passage of time or be reinforced through the thinking process. Although the impact is not so visible, still the ideas of gender stereotypes, ignited within by participating in the workshop, must have changed their way of thinking and perceiving things in future."

Similarly, another collaborator said: "The workshop demonstrates that stereotypes are deeply ingrained but can be challenged through education and empathy. Participants left with a renewed commitment to recognise and overcome their own biases. The collaborative workshop is a resounding success, fostering a collaborative environment for growth and understanding. I am proud to have been a part of this initiative and look forward to future collaborations."

This feedback shows that the project achieved its goals.

Reflection

The current workshop presentation is in English. The pilot practice indicated a language barrier in transmitting the message of the workshop. The collaborator has been translating for a better understanding of the concept. Thus, we are planning to develop at least two more versions; one in Urdu and the second in Chinese either by including captions or audio recording dubbed in the native boli. This may help remove the hurdle faced during pilot practice and may enable the participants to get directly connected with the cognition of the project.

References

Årsvold, C. (2016). Mirror Madness: Investigating Patriarchal Ideology in Versions of "Snow White" [Masters thesis, University of Stavanger, Norway].

Bandura, A. (1988). Organizational Application of Social Cognitive Theory. *Australian Journal of Management*, 13(2), 275–302. doi:10.1177/031289628801300210. S2CID 143104601.

Cekiso, M. (2013). Gender Stereotypes in Selected Fairy Tales: Implications for Teaching Reading in the Foundation Phase in South Africa. *Journal of Sociology and Social Anthropology*, 4(3), 201–206. https://doi.org/10.1080/09766634.2013.11885597

Disney UK. (2018, Nov 21). Ralph Breaks the Internet | She is a Princess Clip | Official Disney UK [Video]. www.youtube.com/watch?v=UNX-8620sDY

Jimenez, S. (2022). The Representation of Women in Disney Animated films. [Bachelor Thesis, University of Nebraska]. https://digitalcommons.unomaha.edu/cgi/viewcontent.cgi?article=1189&context=university_honors_program

Lennon, P. (2021). Language Teaching Methods. In *The Foundations of Teaching English as a Foreign Language* (pp. 31–58). Routledge.

Sharif, U.H. (2016). From Fairy Tales to Disney Movies: Gender Roles and Stereotypes Then and Now. [Master Thesis, BRAC University]. www.academia.edu/73245610/From_fairy_tales_to_disney_movies_gender_roles_and_stereotypes_then_and_now?rhid=27711266409&swp=rr-rw-wc-42120211

UNDP. (2022–2023). Development Advocate Pakistan. www.undp.org/sites/g/files/zskgke326/files/2023-01/genderequality_in_pakistan-climate_politico-economic_stressors.pdf

Veselá, A. (2014). Gender Stereotype in Fairy Tales. [Diploma Thesis, Masaryk University]. https://is.muni.cz/th/365269/pedf_m/Gender_Stereotypes_in_Fairy_Tales.pdf

阿册. (2021). 女性主义视角下的白雪公主与七个小矮人【整理】. 豆瓣(Douban). https://book.douban.com/review/13614502/

庞菲儿. (2020). 改编的颠覆性张力——论电影《沉睡魔咒》的女性主义叙事重构. 东南传播, (10), 62–65. https://doi.org/10.13556/j.cnki.dncb.cn35-1274/j.2020.10.020

鲸落国家二级心理咨询师. (n.d.). 从魔镜的角度分析白雪公主的自体客体发展. 知乎专栏. Retrieved 28 May 2024, from https://zhuanlan.zhihu.com/p/672710514

刘晖玉. (2019). 三个版本《白雪公主》故事的比较研究 (硕士学位论文). 喀什大学.

家有碎娃. (n.d.). 欧洲的黑暗历史，《白雪公主》背后的故事你知道吗？. 知乎专栏. Retrieved 28 May 2024, from https://zhuanlan.zhihu.com/p/268136068

索鋆. (2020). 不再沉默的他者——《沉睡魔咒》中玛琳菲森的声音. 文化学刊, (12), 70–73.

汤素兰. (2024). 公主与女巫的艺术形象演变——以中外经典童话故事为中心. 湘潭大学学报(哲学社会科学版), 48(01), 130–136. https://doi.org/10.13715/j.cnki.jxupss.2024.01.017

张博. (2017). 消解与建构——影片《沉睡魔咒》的女性主义意识透视. 电影评介, (11), 74–76. https://doi.org/10.16583/j.cnki.52-1014/j.2017.11.022

Appendices

Appendix 1. Detailed elaborations of the content in the workshop.

The following appendices will elaborate the content development in each stage.

1. Lead-in

The lead-in stage aims to activate the participants' scheme of the stereotyped princess images in Disney's animated fairy tales and thus draw forth the definition of "gender stereotype". In this stage, the participants will watch a clip (www.youtube.com/watch?v=UNX-8620sDY) and answer the question "What do you think the princess is?". The clip is extracted from *Ralph Breaks the Internet*, and describes a scene in which the leading female character Vanellope encounters the Disney princesses, such as Jasmine, Snow White, and Aurora. Their conversation points out a salient stereotype through the question "Do people assume all your problems get solved because a big strong man showed up?". The clip evokes participants' ideas to answer the question "What do you think the princess is?". The participants could discuss in group or answer individually. From their ideas, the collaborator may point out the existence of gender stereotypes and thus explain what is "gender stereotype".

2. Presentation – *Aladdin*

Presentation stage aims to prepare participants with the frequent gender stereotypes in fairy tales, elaborating three versions of *Aladdin*, i.e., original written version, animated version in 1992, and modern version in 2019.

2.1. The original version

The original version of *Aladdin* is from The Arabian Nights and is a typical stereotyped tale. The video (https://youtu.be/SSdSYk_vuzs?si=WsZadqSFncHrCfhX) elaborates the stereotypes from two selected scenes and points out that the male characters are dominant and the authorities, while the portrayal of the female character is shallow and dependent, her beauty is the only factor that attracts the male (Cekiso, 2013) and she is taken as an object to fulfil the male desire and appreciation.

2.2. The animated version (1992)

The 1992 animated film *Aladdin* demonstrated progress in embracing more feminist ideals and empowered female characters. The video (https://youtu.be/h1ag1JPF2yA?si=tNmb5ntDexD7W_j6) elaborates that in this version, Princess Jasmine is a relatively rich character. She is brave and tries to shape her own destiny. She pursues freedom and is unwilling to be restrained by marriage. Jasmine rejects marrying a Prince, reflecting her independent values and right to choose. When faced with evil, she has some strength to fight back. However, Jasmine's appearance still caters to the traditional model of beauty – slender, large eyes etc. – lacking diversity in representation (Jimenez, 2022). It makes Jasmine's physical attractiveness the important factor in drawing in Aladdin. It devalues Jasmine's inner qualities like personality, intelligence, and abilities. Furthermore, despite her independence, Jasmine is still to be saved and protected by the male hero Aladdin. Aladdin becomes Jasmine's "saviour", reinforcing a masculinist culture, while simplifying the female role to some extent as "waiting to be rescued." Finally, it seems to be a happy ending (Jimenez, 2022). Jasmine gets married since her father revised the law. However, how about her freedom?

2.3. The modern version (2019)

The modern version of *Aladdin* was published in 2019. Compared to the 1992 animated version, this retelling of *Aladdin* presents a Princess Jasmine who is even more strong-minded. The video (https://youtu.be/7FNCMBZlvzg?si=bwMFSm6lBix9q1V2) elaborates that in this version, Jasmine strongly embodies the feminist ideals of empowerment and self-determination. She is outspoken about her desire for equality and power. She boldly confronts her patriarchal society's traditions. In the end, Jasmine becomes the sultan. This ending challenges storytelling that consistently teaches girls their value lies in marrying well, not ruling kingdoms. However, the film still seems not to fully escape deep-rooted gender biases. For example, Jasmine's physical appearance remains bound to conventional assumptions of beauty. There are still no broader representations of the female character. The other female character, Jasmine's handmaid, is thinly sketched without much individual or independent description. She exists mainly to react to and support the leading female character. More problematically, Jasmine still ultimately requires intervention and support from the male hero, Aladdin.

3. Practice – *Snow White*

This stage is mainly to guide the participants to apply the knowledge they just learned about gender stereotypes to analysing three scenes from *Snow White*, and the collaborator will explain the factors and impacts of these stereotypes.

3.1. The readings to interpret *Snow White and the Seven Dwarfs*

The content of this stage is mainly based on the following readings.

One article used Kohut's self-psychology theory to analyse in detail the relationships and psychological states of the characters in *Snow White*. The author points out that the magic mirror in the story is actually a symbol of Snow White's self-object development (鲸落国家二级心理咨询师, n.d.). The magic mirror serves as a tool to reflect the Queen's narcissistic needs, demonstrating the Queen's dependence on satisfying her own grandiose self-needs. In addition, the development process of Snow White also reflects the dynamic changes of the idealised self and the twin self. The author points out that as Snow White grows up, her idealised self develops through identification with the Queen's beauty, but as she herself matures, this identification gradually turns into competition (鲸落国家二级心理咨询师, n.d.). After being expelled to the forest, Snow White's interaction with the seven dwarfs symbolises the development of the twin self. Through labour and interpersonal interactions, Snow White accumulates the skills and strength needed for self-growth (鲸落国家二级心理咨询师, n.d.).

At the same time, if we use a feminist perspective to analyse the role of *Snow White* and the Seven Dwarfs, it is actually a symbol of domestication and labour. Snow White's life with the seven dwarfs symbolises her taming and self-restraint under patriarchy. By serving the dwarfs, Snow White learns important lessons about service, selflessness, and housework, embodying the story's attitude toward "a woman's world and a woman's work": a woman's best role is not only as a member of the family, but as a member who is serving others like a dwarven servant (阿册, 2021).

In addition, Snow White's death is essentially objectifying women. The climax of the story is when Snow White falls into a deep sleep after eating a poisoned apple and is placed in a glass coffin. Her body is objectified and becomes an object of display and desire, symbolising the idealised image of womanhood under patriarchy. This image is eventually "rescued" by the prince, but in fact she will continue to be imprisoned in a male-dominated environment, symbolising that her future destiny is still controlled and possessed (阿册, 2021). Through the analysis of the fairy tale *Snow White*, we can see the complex depiction of female characters in fairy tales and the profound gender cultural connotations behind it. The images of angels and witches created by male authors reflect society's expectations and rejection of women.

Another point that cannot be ignored is the prototype of the seven dwarfs, that is, the historical background of child labour in the Middle Ages. In the early 19th century, British industry developed rapidly, and the demand for labour in factories and mines increased sharply. According to historical records, on June 8, 1835, a gas explosion occurred in the Wallsend Mine near Newcastle, killing 101 miners, 75 of whom were child labourers. This incident caused widespread concern and shock in society. Similarly, on July 4, 1838, 26 children died, including 11 girls, the youngest of whom was just seven years old, when a creek flooded the Skerstone Colliery in South Yorkshire after a continuous thunderstorm (家有碎娃, n.d.). These accidents highlight the extremely dangerous working conditions for children in mines. The problem of child labour is not limited to the Industrial Revolution. In medieval Europe, child labour was also common in cities. In medieval England, every home had a fireplace for heating, and the narrow chimneys needed to be swept regularly. Since chimney space was limited, small children, known as chimney sweeps, were often hired to do the job. This dangerous and unhygienic work posed a great threat to the health and safety of children (家有碎娃, n.d.).

3.2. Three scenes from *Snow White*

The three scenes from *Snow White* present typical stereotypes and are effective practice for the participants in recognising the stereotyped features.

In the first scene, the Queen wants to kill Snow White because she is more beautiful than her. Therefore, beauty is the keynote throughout the story, and the appearance competition between women reflects the requirement of women's pursuit of beautiful appearance.

In the second act, Snow White said that in order to stay in the seven dwarfs' home, she would wash, clean, mend, and cook for them, and would also remind the seven dwarfs to wash their hands before eating. Taking care of men and living dependently on men as the main expectation for women is the female gender stereotype in the second act.

The third gender stereotype is that women need to rely on men to live a happy life. Women are weak, lack the ability to be autonomous, and always need the protection of men, which in turn strengthens the dominant role of men to a certain extent. At the end of the story, Snow White and the prince were together, and they lived a happy life. The story ends with a wedding, conveying that women's goal in life is marriage. This simplified ending and superficial understanding is based on stereotypes and biased views of gender roles, which at once emphasises that women should be submissive to men and should focus on family matters.

3.3. Analysing the historical context

After identifying the stereotypes, participants will explore the historical context to enhance their understanding.

Snow White is a fairy tale created by the Brothers Grimm in 1812. German society was in a period of turmoil. Therefore, the role of the Queen is actually the embodiment of a cruel and tyrannical ruler. When faced with her jealousy towards Snow White, she did not hesitate to issue an order to kill her. This way of consolidating one's status was very cruel, reflecting the society's aversion to tyranny and autocratic rule at that time, as well as people's desire to fight against this form of rule (Årsvold, 2016).

Since Germany was in the early stages of industrialisation at that time, the demand for minerals began to increase, so labour became a big problem. Slave labour became popular. Many of the slaves working in these mines were child slaves, so the seven dwarfs actually correspond to children who had to join the labour force due to social oppression at that time (阿册, 2021).

3.4. Analysing the social factors

Within the understanding of the above historical context, the participants are supposed to consider what social factors shape Snow White's character and the development of the plot.

When creating the characters of *Snow White*, there was no doubt that it was in line with the patriarchal thinking of the time. Due to the status of women in German society at that time, women had very limited opportunities to go out to study and work. Therefore, compared to participating in activities in the public sphere, women assumed family responsibilities. This is why Snow White has skills such as washing clothes, cooking, sweeping the floor, etc. The princess has a noble status, and having such skills may conflict with her status, but this contradiction is in line with the social thinking of the time and people's expectations for women at the time (Årsvold, 2016).

The plot of *Snow White* being awakened by the prince is based on the fact that men are often the main body of society. Compared with powerful men, women can only perform housework activities and live a life dependent on men, resulting in their inability to be independent. This social reality strengthens the solidification of gender roles and weakens women's autonomy and independence (Årsvold, 2016).

3.5. Analysis of the prince

This stage also draws participants' attention to discussing the prince image in *Snow White*. The analysis of the prince image will consequently strengthen participants' awareness of stereotypes towards female characters.

The prince's attraction stems primarily from Snow White's beauty. This reflects that women are often objectified in traditional stories, and their appearance becomes their main or even only capital for gaining attention and love. The value of female characters is reduced to outer beauty rather than inner qualities or abilities. Men have the initiative and superiority to choose their partners.

Symbolically, the image of the prince represents the ideal male role under patriarchy. His appearance and behaviour conform to traditional society's expectations of men: protector, redeemer, and decider. This kind of role setting is not only common in fairy tales, but also affects the concept of relationships between men and women in real society to a certain extent (阿册, 2021).

4. Production – *Maleficent*

This stage prominently employs the comparison between animation *Sleeping Beauty* and its retold version *Maleficent* to guide and encourage the participants to reimagine the ending of *Snow White*, thus, challenging the gender stereotypes.

4.1. *Sleeping Beauty* (1959): the original animation

First, this stage employs a clip from *Sleeping Beauty* to discuss the stereotyped female characters.

They are relatively one-dimensional, that is, Princess Aurora and Maleficent representing pure good and evil respectively. This simplification of characters contributes to the reinforcement of traditional gender roles and stereotypes. Also, the portrayal of the princess is as passive and helpless. Aurora, the titular character, spends much of the story asleep, waiting for a prince to come and rescue her. This reinforces a stereotype that women are dependent on men for their happiness and safety.

4.2. *Maleficent* (2014): the modern retelling version

The participants will then watch a clip from *Maleficent* to discuss the alternative portrayal of female characters.

Maleficent offers a fascinating reimagining of the classic *Sleeping Beauty* from a feminist perspective. In the original story, Maleficent is portrayed as a one-dimensional villain whose motivations are never fully explored. However, in this modern retelling, the character of Maleficent is humanised, and her actions are contextualised within a narrative that challenges traditional gender roles and stereotypes.

One of the most significant departures from the original tale is the exploration of Maleficent's backstory and her complex relationship with Princess Aurora. Rather than being driven solely by jealousy or malevolence, Maleficent's actions are depicted as a response to betrayal and injustice, highlighting themes of female empowerment and agency. By providing depth and nuance to Maleficent's character, the film subverts the stereotype of the evil, power-hungry witch and instead presents her as a nuanced and sympathetic figure.

4.3. The comparison between *Sleeping Beauty* and *Maleficent*

Using the two versions, the collaborators will guide the participants to explore the differences between them.

i) Empowerment vs. dependency

In *Sleeping Beauty*, the resolution relies on Prince Phillip's kiss to awaken Aurora, emphasising her passive role in her own awakening and ultimate rescue. This reinforces the stereotype of women as helpless and dependent on male intervention for their salvation.

In contrast, *Maleficent* subverts this trope by having Maleficent herself break the curse with a kiss of maternal love. This empowers Maleficent as the primary agent of Aurora's awakening, challenging the notion of female passivity and dependency on male rescuers.

ii) Romantic love vs. maternal love

The ending of *Sleeping Beauty* highlights romantic love as the key to Aurora's happiness, with her ultimate fulfillment achieved through her marriage to Prince Phillip. This perpetuates the idea that a woman's worth is tied to her ability to find a suitable male partner.

Conversely, *Maleficent* prioritises maternal love over romantic love, as it is Maleficent's love for Aurora that ultimately saves her from the curse. This redefines the notion of true love beyond romantic relationships and emphasises the importance of familial bonds and non-romantic forms of love.

iii) Prince as hero vs. collaboration

In *Sleeping Beauty*, Prince Phillip is depicted as the heroic figure who rescues Aurora and defeats the evil Maleficent. This reinforces traditional gender roles, where men are portrayed as strong, assertive, and the primary agents of action.

Maleficent challenges this stereotype by portraying Prince Phillip as a supportive ally rather than the primary hero. He works alongside Maleficent and Aurora to defeat the true villain, highlighting the importance of collaboration and mutual respect between genders.

4.4. The retelling of the ending of *Snow White*

After discussing the adaptation of *Sleeping Beauty*, it is worth encouraging the participants to retell the ending of *Snow White*.

Appendix 2. Handout for participants.

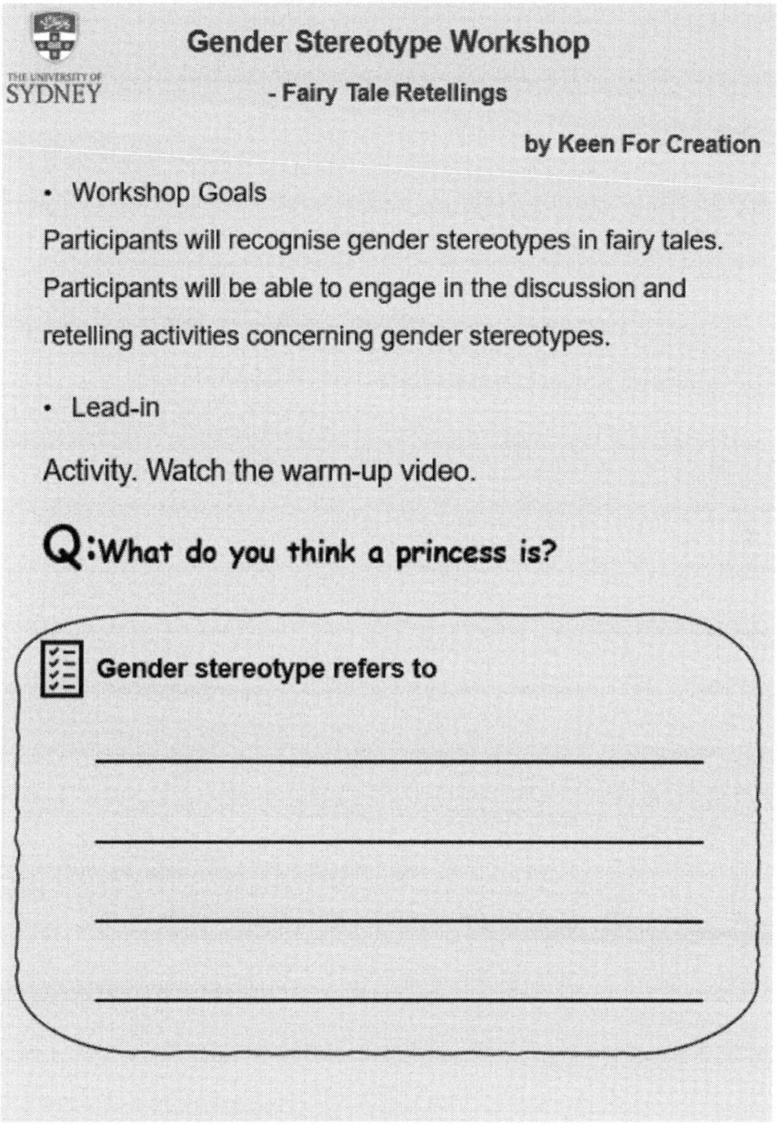

SYDNEY — THE UNIVERSITY OF

Gender Stereotype Workshop
- Fairy Tale Retellings

by Keen For Creation

- Workshop Goals

Participants will recognise gender stereotypes in fairy tales. Participants will be able to engage in the discussion and retelling activities concerning gender stereotypes.

- Lead-in

Activity. Watch the warm-up video.

Q: What do you think a princess is?

Gender stereotype refers to

_____

_____

_____

_____

Figure 13.4 Page 1 of Handout for participants

170 Subaltern Linguistics

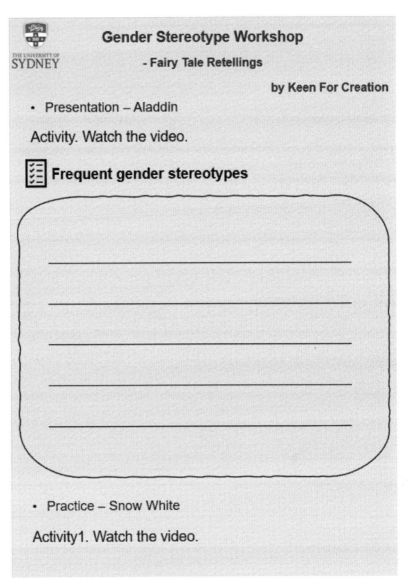

Figure 13.5 Page 2 of Handout for participants

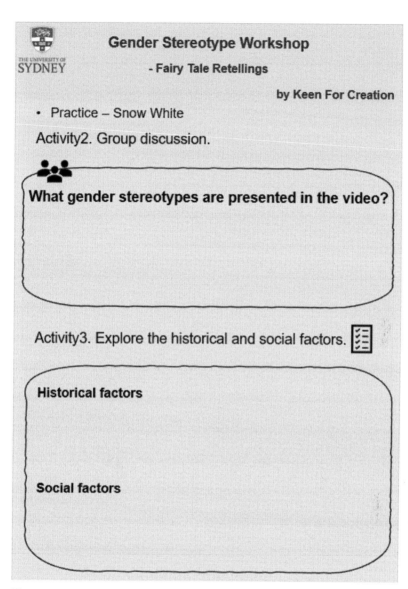

Figure 13.6 Page 3 of Handout for participants

172 Subaltern Linguistics

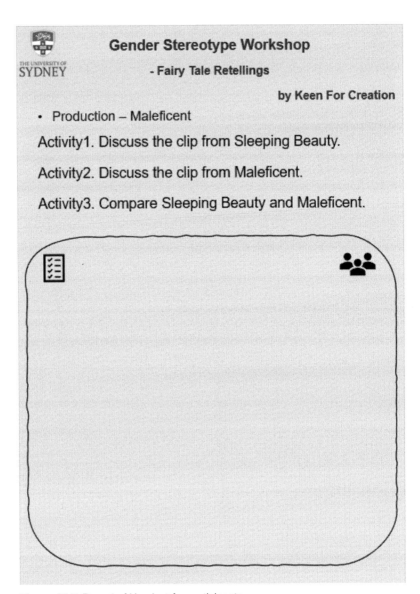

Figure 13.7 Page 4 of Handout for participants

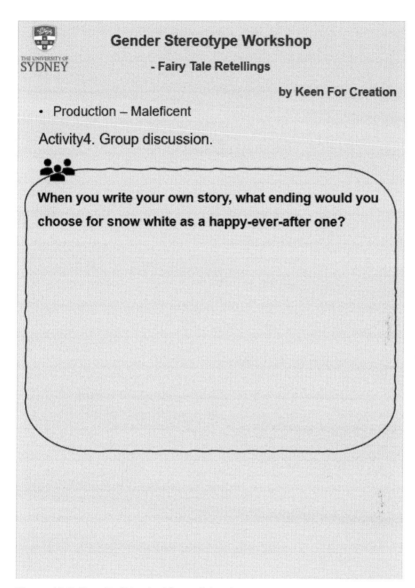

Figure 13.8 Page 5 of Handout for participants

174 Subaltern Linguistics

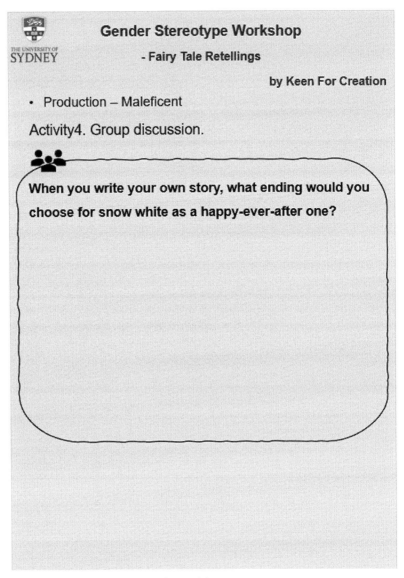

Figure 13.9 Page 6 of Handout for participants

Appendix 3. Results of handouts for pilot practice

www.routledge.com/9781032800325

Appendix 4. Photos and videos of the pilot practice

www.routledge.com/9781032800325

176 Subaltern Linguistics

Appendix 5

Figure 13.10 Copy of Body Safety Australia flyer used for PDA

14 Cantonese dialect maintenance among children

Jianying Huang, Qintang Yu, and Mengling Zhao

Introduction

As a part of the Guangdong Cultural area, Dongguan City is in the coastal area of Guangdong Province, China. Nowadays, many children are not acquainted with Cantonese and its culture. Some parents have complained about their own children speaking Cantonese less than Mandarin. The project focuses on teaching 4th to 6th-grade students in the Guangdong region to read ancient Chinese poetry using Cantonese. This initiative includes online courses and a painting collection activity, designed to deepen students' appreciation of their cultural heritage while improving their language skills in Cantonese. Therefore, this report includes the key components of the project: links to online resources, credibility analysis of assessment of context, needs, engagement and benefits, literature review of relevant research, Positive Discourse Analysis (PDA) insights, the material development process, implementation details, reflections on successes and areas for improvement, references from all sources, and appendices to additional materials.

Material

WeChat Tweet Publicity's Original Link: https://a.xiumi.us/board/v5/6yL2l/532246810

Video Recording of Cantonese Teaching Lesson:
https://meeting.tencent.com/v2/cloud-record/share?id=06cf7c7b-29af-4e04-aa5f2b63958b331c&from=3&record_type=2

Cantonese Teaching PowerPoint: See Appendix A (Figure 14.3)

Posters (see Figures 14.1 and 14.2):

Figure 14.1 Cantonese Teaching Poem Class advertisement

Figure 14.2 Collecting Guangdong Morning Tea's Paintings

Establishing credibility

Context: the project addresses the preservation and revitalisation of Cantonese, a vital local dialect in Guangdong, by incorporating it into educational practices.

Real-world need: there is a significant need to maintain cultural heritage and language diversity. This project fulfills this by making ancient Chinese poetry accessible and relevant to young Cantonese speakers.

Engagement and stakeholders: local schools, parents, and cultural institutions in China's Dongguan city are engaged as primary stakeholders, ensuring the project is community-cantered and supported.

Domestic/local knowledge and understandings used: the project leverages local knowledge from various studies and practical explorations in Cantonese teaching. Research by Huang (2011) and Zhou et al. (2020) highlights effective factors and innovative practices in language acquisition and teaching. Additionally, the curriculum is based on local dialects and cultural contexts, making it relatable and easier for students to grasp.

International perspectives: while the focus is local, the project's approach to language education could be shared internationally, offering insights into effective dialect-based education methods. International perspectives are integrated through comparative studies and pedagogical insights from global educational practices. Research by Wong and Johnston (2004) and Özgen (2004) provides insights into language development and perception, crucial for designing an effective curriculum. Pan (2021) and Pearce et al. (2019) offer models for incorporating cultural elements into language learning, emphasising the importance of holistic educational approaches.

Benefits of the work: students not only learn about their cultural heritage but also improve their linguistic skills in Cantonese, enhancing their cognitive flexibility, and cultural literacy. In addition, this project fosters a sense of community and cultural pride among participants and provides educators with innovative tools and methods for effective teaching.

Lead features of the work: innovative teaching methods such as interactive online platforms and localised content, which are tailored to the young audience's engagement styles.

Ethical dimensions considered: the project promotes linguistic diversity and cultural preservation, crucial in the face of globalisation. It respects and elevates the local dialect, ensuring it continues to be a vibrant part of the community's identity.

Analysis of literature

Pearce, Nichols, and Erlam's "The Power of the Poem: Exploring the Use of Poetry in the Beginner Languages Classroom" demonstrates considerable interest in the study of poetry in language schools. This article highlights the benefits of poetry in language learning, especially for beginners. This innovative approach emphasises how poetic expression can improve learners' linguistic competence, cultural sensitivity, and emotional engagement. Teachers can use the rhythm and rich expression of poetry to effectively help children master vocabulary, phonological awareness, and intonation. This approach can deepen connections with the language and its cultural nuances, which is particularly important for teaching Cantonese to young learners in the Guangdong region.

Moreover, according to the approach of Zhou, Peng, and Liang (2020), Cantonese training should be more interesting and engaging for younger students to increase their motivation and interest in learning the language. This approach is closely related to the objective of the CREDIBLE project, which is to deepen the appreciation and fluency of Cantonese culture among students in grades four to six. It includes creative teaching techniques, culturally resonant content, and engaging activities tailored to the cognitive and socio-emotional needs of young learners. This paper provides valuable insights into creating an effective and enjoyable learning experience for this CREDIBLE program.

In addition, Chen (2023) studied the application of Cantonese chanting in the teaching of Tang poetry. Cantonese chanting is a kind of recited text with rhythm and melody. It is often used for reciting opera, poetry and other traditional Chinese cultures. Chen's research explores how to make Tang poetry more accessible and enjoyable for students to learn with Cantonese chanting. This approach incorporates the storytelling techniques, tone, and cultural components characteristic of Cantonese chanting. Therefore, Chen's research attempts to foster a deeper knowledge and appreciation of both the language and cultural components of these literary works by incorporating Cantonese chanting into the teaching of Tang poetry has also inspired this CREDIBLE project.

For age selection, Wong & Johnston (2004) conducted experiments to observe referential skills in different age groups, providing valuable insights into the development of these skills. The results show that children aged 10–12 demonstrate a significant improvement in their ability to use clear reference in speech. This discovery supports our selection of the target audience and emphasises that our project is suitable for students in grades 4 to 6. By understanding the stages of referential development, our program can adjust its educational approach to effectively improve the language skills of children in this age group.

Last but not least, Zhang and Liu's (2018) practical investigation focused on dialect instruction in a community education setting using an omnimedia environment. This article highlights two terms: "omnimedia" and "omnimedia environment". The term "omnimedia" describes how different media platforms and technologies are integrated into the learning environment. In this study, Zhang and Liu examined the best ways to teach languages such as Cantonese through community education programs, considering participants' different learning styles and requirements. The use of interactive platforms, multimedia materials, and community engagement technologies are all included. The term "omnimedia environment" then refers to an all-encompassing strategy that leverages digital technologies, traditional instructional techniques, and community engagement to improve dialect learning outcomes. This strategy involves interactive materials made specifically for the linguistic and cultural context of the community, workshops, online courses, and cultural events.

By drawing inspiration from these literature sources, this CREDIBLE project integrates innovative teaching methods, online platforms, and localised content in order to engage young learners effectively.

Positive Discourse Analysis

In developing this project on maintaining the Cantonese dialect among children, inspiration was drawn from multiple sources, each contributing unique insights that enhanced this project's effectiveness and relevance.

Firstly, Pearce, Nichols, and Erlam (2019) were instrumental in shaping this project's methodology. This article emphasised the pedagogical benefits of using poetry to teach languages, highlighting its ability to foster linguistic fluency, cultural sensitivity, and emotional engagement. The rhythmic and expressive nature of poetry was shown to aid in vocabulary retention, phonetic accuracy, and cultural appreciation. Inspired by this, the group integrated ancient Chinese poetry into the Cantonese language curriculum for 4th to 6th grade students. By leveraging the poetic form, the group aimed to create a dynamic and immersive learning experience, making the language more accessible and engaging for young learners.

The second inspiration came from a bilibili video featuring the famous Chinese host Sa Beining, who recited a poem in Cantonese. This short yet impactful video showcased the captivating power of a well-executed recitation. Sa Beining's performance was both powerful and engaging, demonstrating how the tonal and rhythmic qualities of Cantonese poetry differ markedly from Mandarin. The familiarity of the poem he recited resonated with many viewers, highlighting the importance of choosing culturally significant and well-known pieces for language teaching. This led us to incorporate the same poem into the teaching materials, using it to illustrate the distinct phonetic patterns of Cantonese and to captivate the students' interest. The video underscored the effectiveness of multimedia tools in enhancing language learning, prompting the group members to include video content in the course to make sessions more engaging and to maintain students' attention.

Additionally, the article by Zhou, Peng, and Liang (2020) provided valuable strategies to sustain students' interest and engagement in learning Cantonese. The article highlighted techniques such as incorporating games, storytelling, and multimedia resources into lessons to make learning more enjoyable and effective. Drawing from these strategies, the group members designed the course to include various interactive elements and multimedia content to capture and sustain the students' interest, ensuring a more dynamic and engaging learning experience.

Finally, Zhang and Liu's (2018) article provided the group with a framework for utilising modern educational technologies and community engagement in dialect preservation. This article emphasised the importance of integrating local dialect teaching within a community context, supported by multimedia tools. Drawing from these insights, the group collaborated with local educational institutions and incorporated multimedia resources, such as interactive courseware and video content, to create a comprehensive and engaging learning environment for the students.

The use of culturally relevant poetry and multimedia tools made the learning experience more engaging and effective. The rhythmic and expressive qualities of poetry, combined with the captivating power of video recitations, enhanced students' linguistic skills and cultural appreciation. By integrating chanting techniques and leveraging community resources, the group created a dynamic and immersive educational environment that not only preserved the Cantonese dialect but also fostered a deeper connection to cultural heritage. These elements taught us the importance of incorporating diverse and interactive teaching methods, ultimately helping the group develop a more effective and engaging Cantonese language education program for young learners.

Material development

Based on the previous research on the current situation of Cantonese among young people, and the feedback from interviews with parents of some of the young people, the goals and objectives of the project were established.

The target of the project is students in grades 4–6 in Dongguan, Guangdong Province, who are unfamiliar with Cantonese and are interested in participating in the program, which is divided into two parts. In the first part, we have chosen to teach the online Cantonese poem in which students can recite the Cantonese poem with correct Cantonese pronunciation. In the second part, we will collect paintings of Cantonese Morning Tea from painting organisations' students to see the perspective and depth of the students' understanding of Cantonese Morning Tea.

Ancient poems are taught in Cantonese to promote students' understanding and inheritance of traditional Chinese culture and to strengthen their sense of identity in the traditional culture of the Guangdong region. By studying ancient poems, students will improve their Cantonese listening and speaking skills and enhance their ability to perceive and apply the language, especially in literature and classical languages.

The project chose two collaborators to achieve our campaign. Both are organisations specifically dedicated to Primary students' education. One is a professional educational institution in Dongguan, Guangdong Province, another is an independent private art institution that educates students of all ages interested in calligraphy and painting.

After several drafts and revisions, the lectures were conducted in an online format, and the content of the lectures was to teach the participating students to read aloud the Cantonese version of 'On the Stork Tower'. The lectures were conducted in the form of PPTs and constructed using text, pictures, audio, and video. At the same time, we set Q&A sessions and invited volunteer follow-up sessions to have more effective interaction with students, and set some prizes to encourage their engagement. The other part was to collect some drawings of Cantonese dim sum that were solicited from the students in the studio to evoke their interest in Cantonese dim sum.

The team chose to adopt the traditional publicity methods that parents of students are more accustomed to for the promotion tactics of this event. The first was to design two posters for the two events, which were placed in the parent groups and official WeChat accounts of the partner organisations. The second was to use WeChat tweets to introduce and promote the two events in detail.

Advice to others who want to develop similar projects is to do enough research in the early stage, clarify market status and available resources, determine the target audience, and then start the specific preparatory work. In developing our project, we also realised the importance of having strong collaborators on board - people who believe in and support the work. In addition, we also met a number of problems during material development and found that our collaborators and colleagues had good advice. We recommend that project developers be open to feedback and, in fact, solicit comments and suggestions as they develop their work. Feedback helps improve material and project outcomes.

Implementation

The project focuses on Cantonese poetry teaching and Cantonese cultural painting. We produced online course materials and released posters seeking paintings. We cooperated with the Lotus Umbrella Reading Organisation (Collaborator 1) and Big Red Kai Art Studio

(Collaborator 2) in Dongguan City, Guangdong Province, China. These institutions not only have extensive experience and resources in children's education but also provide courses in traditional dialects. The Cantonese poetry teaching offers an online course to 12 children aged 10–12 from collaborator 1. The project-designed courseware and teaching methods allow students to read a poem in Cantonese in this class and encourage them to use Cantonese for reciting poetry or communicating. The Cantonese cultural painting activity involves designing a poster for collecting artworks and providing painting materials to Partner 2, encouraging younger children to explore Cantonese culture through painting. After launching the poster and course, the project has received many children's homework and artwork, as well as useful feedback from parents and teachers. Some parents believe their children use Cantonese in life and school, but others worry that the course doesn't change much.

Reflection

The main goal of this project is to offer students the opportunity to learn how to recite ancient poetry in Cantonese through this online class. Even though the classes have been running smoothly, there are still a number of parts that could use some improvement. First is the method of online teaching. As a result of the fact that many parents are concerned about their children's screen time, they do not entirely agree that online classes can help students learn languages. Second is class interaction. The question-and-answer format still results in quiet and boring sessions, which fails to engage all students actively. In addition, online teaching greatly limits the possibilities and space for setting up classroom activities. If the project is to be further refined, offline classes are a better choice for teaching Cantonese and various forms of classroom games could be inserted in the class. Furthermore, the project could be organised into a systematic teaching framework, divided into 2–3 lesson units, such as pronunciation training and the use of Cantonese romanisation.

References

Chen, C. (2023). Yueyu yinsong zai Tangshi jiaoxue Zhong de yunyong [Research on the application of Cantonese recitation in the teaching of Tang poetry]. *Popular Literature and Art*, (20), 200–202. doi:10.20112/j.cnki.ISSN1007-5828.2023.20.066

Huang, J. (2011). Yingxiang ertong yuyan xide de yinsu yanjiu [Research on factors affecting children's language acquisition]. *Science and Education Wenhui*, (16), 125–126.

Özgen, E. (2004). Language, learning, and color perception. *Current Directions in Psychological Science*, 13(3), 95–98. www.jstor.org/stable/20182921

Pan, Y. (2021). Integrating Cantonese nursery rhymes into early childhood music classrooms: A lesson for learning music, language, and culture. *Journal of General Music Education*, 35(1), 34–45.

Pearce, N., Nichols, J., & Erlam, R. (2019). The Power of the Poem: Exploring the use of Poetry in the Beginner Languages Classroom. *Babel (Parkville, Australia)*, 53(3), 22.

Wong, A.M.-Y., & Johnston, J.R. (2004). The development of discourse referencing in Cantonese-speaking children. *Journal of Child Language*, 31(3), 633–660. doi:10.1017/S030500090400604X

Zhang, G., & Liu, L. (2018). Quanmeiti huanjing xia shequ jiaoyu fangyan jiaoxue de Shijian tansuo——Yi Yueyu weili [Practical exploration of dialect teaching in community education in an all-media environment—taking Cantonese as an example]. *Journal of Guangzhou Radio and Television University*, 4.

Zhou, Y., Peng, F., & Liang, J. (2020). Zengtian Yueyu jiaoxue meili, Tigao xuesheng xuexi xingqu [Adding charm to Cantonese teaching and improving students' interest in learning]. Writers' World.

Appendix A

Figure 14.3 Cantonese teaching PowerPoint

Appendix B

PDA of Sa Beining's Cantonese version of "Ascending Stork Building"

Table 14.1

	Description	What meanings are being projected?
Sight	Pictures, paintings or image	The images on the courseware and posters make the project less serious and boring for students and parents.
	Cantonese characters and Cantonese-pinyin	The characters on the courseware let students understand the difference between Chinese pinyin and Cantonese Pinyin.
	Video on Wechat post	Video insertion in the classroom allows students to pay more attention and enriches class sessions.
Sound	Reciting a poem in Cantonese	By reading poems repeatedly, students can memorise and repeat the Cantonese pronunciation.
Smell	N/A	N/A
Touch	N/A	N/A
Taste	Artworks about dim sums	Dim sum, a symbol of Cantonese culture on posters, can evoke students' taste for Cantonese cuisine.

Index

Note: Figures are shown in *italics* and tables in **bold** type.

Aboriginal Ways of Learning (Eight Ways) pedagogy 48–50, *49*, *50*, *51*
academia 4, 6, 12, 14, 17, 21, 30
action and continuity 83, 85, 99, 111, 117
activity sheet, for Kids Guide to Art in Camden project 123, 125–126, 127, *127*, 128, *128*, 129, *129*, 130, *134*, *135*
affective colouring 137
AITSL (Australian Institute for Teaching and School Leadership) 46, 47
Aladdin 151–152, 154, 155, **158**, *158*, 162–163
Alan Baker Art Gallery 124, 129–130, *129*
analysis of literature 124–125, 137–139, 153–154, 179–181; *see also How to Write: A Literature Review for Project Development*; literature review
apprenticeship 7, 8
APST (Australian Professional Standards for Teachers) 46
art spaces 123, 124, 125, 127, 128, 130
assessment 6, 7, 8, 14, 41, 177; *see also* evaluation
Australian anti-tobacco campaign 31, 32–35, *33*, **34**
Australian Institute for Teaching and School Leadership (AITSL) 46, 47
Australian Professional Standards for Teachers (APST) 46

beliefs 3, 4, 14, 15, 18, 20, 28, *31*, 41; that mistakes are bad 149; societal 151; socio-semiotic 21
Benefits local communities, element of CREDIBLE approach *31*, 31, 35, 36, 38, 39, 40, 92, **118**, 124, 137, 153, 179
big groups 140, 141
bilibili video 181
"Bins for the Future" 63–64, *64*, *65*
blogs 138–139
Body Safety Australia *176*
boli 1, 13; and borrowing from English 11; documenting of 21–22; for naming 16; is science 11; for sorting 16; technicalising of 7–9; and writing systems 9–11, *10*, 28
broad Positive Discourse Analysis (broad PDA) 32, 33, **34**, 51, 88, 89, 90; of Garbage Sorting project 104–105; of The Ribbit-Ribbit Pond 93, **93**, 95; template for 114, **115–116**
brochure, for Overseas Student Health Cover project 68, *68*
"Burramatta" 126

Cabramatta Intensive English Centre (IEC) 46, 48, 50
Camden Visitor Information Centre 126, *126*, 129
Camden walking tours and maps 125, *126*
campaigns: analysis template for 88–89, **89**, **107**, **108**, **115**; Australian anti-tobacco 31,

32–35, *33*, **34**, 88; endometriosis health 72–73; Overseas Student Health Cover 67, 68, *68*, 69; reusable coffee cups 62, *62*, 63

Cantonese: chanting 180; culture 177, 180, 182–183, 184, **187**; dialect maintenance 177–184, *178*; Garbage Sorting project 60–61, 108, 110; 177, 178, 181, 183, 184

card deck 140, 141, 142, **148**

Card Game: Kings 146, **147**; Story-Builder 139–140, 147–148, **148**; Try-Out and Feedback 148–150, *149*

Cards for Courage 136–142

categorisation 11, 15, 16–18, 19–20; The Trash Project 71, 72; *see also* classification

CDA (Critical Discourse Analysis) 32, 88

Cherokee syllabary 9, 35–36, *35*

child labour 164–165

Chinese language 9, 111, 148, 160

Chinese Pinyin 60, **187**

choose to reuse 43, 59, 61–63, *62*

classification 11, 15, 16–17, **23**, 71, 104; *see also* categorisation

coffee cups 43, 59, 61–63, *62*

collaboration 59, 63, 64, 69, 86, 87, 103, 114, 115, 151; Cantonese Dialect Maintenance project 183–184; Cards for Courage project 136, 140, 141–142, 145–146; Gender Stereotypes in Fairy Tales project 155, 158, 159, 160, 162, 167–168

colonial knowledge 18, 22, 24, 26

colonial sciences 15, 16, 17, 18

colonial socio-semiotics 5, 20

colonisation 4, 5–6, 7, 14, 15, 18, 25–26, 36, 74, 81

colour 22, 156

colouring book *60*, 60, 108, *109*, **110**, 111

commonsense knowledge 138

community engagement 181, 182

community socio-semiotics 85

conceptualisation, stage of CREDIBLE projects 5, 83, 85–87, *86*, 97, 102–103, *103*, 114, *114*, 115

confidence: linguistic 90, 92, 137, 138–139, 141–142, 145; in public speaking 140, 148

Contextually relevant, element of CREDIBLE approach 30–31, *31*, 34, 36, 38, 40, 90, 91, 124, 137, 151, 152, 178

credibility 31; establishing 124, 137, 152–153, 178–179

CREDIBLE approach 1, 4–5, 30–32, *31*; *see also* Australian anti-tobacco campaign; Cherokee syllabary; "Free Throw Plastic Bottles" Smiling Mind meditation app

CREDIBLE projects: for economic development 74–81, **75**, **76**, **77**, **79**, **80**; for education 45–58, *47*, *49*, *50*, *51*, *52*, *53*, *54*, *55*, *56*, *57*; for the environment 59–64, *60*, *61*, *62*, *64*, *65*; for health and wellbeing 66–73, *67*, *68*, *69*, *70*, *71*

CREDIBLE report template **118–119**

Critical Discourse Analysis (CDA) 32, 88

culture 5, 24, 36, *49*, *75*, *77*, *78*, 81; Cantonese 177, 180, 182–183, 184, **187**; masculinist 162–163

curricula 3, 25, 41, 48, 137, 138, 141, 179, 181

data analysis 83, 87–90, **89**, 103–105, *104*, *105*, 115

deck of cards 140, 141, 142, **148**

Deconstruction 52, *52*, 53

dependency 168; socio-semiotic 27

designing things form 95, **96**, 97, 97–98, 99, 108, **110–111**, **112**, 114, **116–117**

destructive goals 27

dialect instruction 180–181

dialects 9, 30; Cantonese 177–184, *178*

Index

discomfort, with leading experiences in gallery space 123, 125
disempowerment 10, 25
dissemination 5, 121, 152
division 17; socio-semiotics of 27
documentation 22, 76–77, 99, 111, 113, 117–119, **118–119**
domestic familiarity 153
Draws on an understanding of local knowledge and practices, element of CREDIBLE approach 31, 35, 36, 39, 40, 66

EAL/D (English as an Additional Language or Dialect) 46, 48, *49*
economic benefits, of Language Travels 77–78
economic development 25; CREDIBLE projects for 74–81, *75*, *76*, *77*, *79*, *80*
economy 4, 8, 26, 41, 91; micro- 21, 75, 78
educating on garbage sorting 43, 59–61, *60*, *61*
education: to achieve independence 26; CREDIBLE projects for 45–58, *47*, *49*, *50*, *51*, *52*, *53*, *54*, *55*, *56*, *57*; Indigenous 13; literacy as goal of 6–7; literacy-based 9–10; modern-colonial 3–4; in pre-colonial period 8
educational institutions 25–26, 182, 183
educational policies 25
educational systems 25–26
Eight Ways (Aboriginal Ways of Learning) pedagogy 48–50, *49*, *50*, *51*
emotional engagement 179, 181
employment 4, 6, 25, 33
empowerment 30, 38, 39, 41, 73, 74, 77–78, 87, 130, 152, 168; dis- 10, 25; female 152, 162, 163, 167, 168
endangered languages 74
endometriosis health campaign 72–73
engagement 7, 14, 25, 26, 28, 47, 90, 123, 140, 146, **147**, 177; in Cantonese 181–182, 183; community 181, 182; emotional 179, 181
Engages stakeholders, element of CREDIBLE approach *31*, 35, 36, 38–39, 40, 91, **118**, 124, 137, 152–153, 178–179
English as Additional Language or Dialect (EAL/D) 46, 48, *49*
English education, in non-English speaking countries 136
English language 8, 9, 11, 12, 16, 26, 27, 28
environment, CREDIBLE projects for the 59–64, *60*, *61*, *62*, *64*, *65*
environmental sustainability 102
epistemologies 15, 30
establishing credibility 124, 137, 152–153, 178–179
Ethical dimensions, element of CREDIBLE approach *31*, 31, 35, 36, 39, 40, **92**, **118**, 124, 137, 153, 179
evaluation 12, 14, 99, 113, **119**, 130, 138; *see also* assessment

fairy tales, gender stereotypes in 151–160, *156*, *157*, **158**
fake news 8, 27
fear of holding the group back 141
fear of making mistakes 136, 138, 139, 140, 141, 142, 150
female characters 151, 154, 162, 163, 164, 166, 167
female empowerment 152, 162, 163, 167, 168
feminism 162, 163, 164, 167
finite category 15, 17, 18
fixed mindset 138–139
FLC (Free Linguistic Conference) website 72, 75, 99, 101
flyers *80*, *156*, *156*, *157*, *176*
free art spaces 123
Free Linguistics Conference (FLC) 21–22, 74, 75, 78, *80*, 81; website 72, 75, 99, 101
Free Throw Plastic Bottles 39–41, *40*
future tense 27

gallery spaces 123, 125, 130
gamification 136, 137, 138, 139
garbage sorting, educating on 43, 59–61, *60*, *61*
Gauci, Regan 45, 46
gender bias 151, 152, 163
Gender equity and inclusion Professional Development workshop 156
gender roles 152, 153, 154, 165, 166, 167, 168
gender stereotypes, in fairy tales 151–160, *156*, *157*, **158**
genealogy 16, 17
goals 27; of broad PDA 32; of CREDIBLE approach *see* goals of CREDIBLE approach; of education 6–7, 26, 41; of anything in 'infinite' category 17, 18; literacy as 6–7; of projects *53*, *55*, *57*, 86, 88
goals: of Cards for Courage project 146, 147; of CREDIBLE projects 103; destructive 27; of garbage sorting project **110**; and Positive Discourse Analysis (PDA) 32, **89**, **93**, **96**; project *53*, *55*, *57*, 109, 114; of The Ribbit-Ribbit Pond **97**, **98**; of supporting online teaching project 48; unachievable 18; waste sorting poster **106**
Gonzalez, Ivan 21, 86, 90, 93, **93**, **97**
government policies 104
grammar 9, 10, 13, 22, 40, 52, 77, 78, 136, 145
Group A sensory systems **23**, 23, 24, 25
Group B sensory systems **23**, 23, 24
growth mindset 138, 139

handouts 153, 156, 157–158, 159, *169*, *170*, *171*, *172*, *173*, *174*, 175
health, CREDIBLE projects for 66–73, *67*, *68*, *69*, *70*, *71*
healthcare 4, 66, 67
Hindi 28
historical context 151–152, 165–166
Ħobż biż-żejt *50*, *51*

How to Write: A Literature Review for Project Development 46, 50, *53*, *55*, 55, 57
How to Write: Receiving and Admission Nursing Notes 46, 50, 52, 53, *54*, 56
"How to Write…" workbooks 50–58, *51*, *52*, *53*, *54*, *55*, *56*, *57*

ICC (Intercultural Communicative Competence) 86–87, 90–92, **91–92**, **93**, **97**
implementation: of Cantonese dialect maintenance project 183–184; of Cards for Courage project 141–142; with collaborators 59, 85; of CREDIBLE projects 99; of Gender Stereotypes in Fairy Tales project 159–160; of Kids Guide to Art in Camden project 129–130, *129*; pre- 99, **117**
independence 4, 25, 26, 162, 166
Independent Construction 52, 56, 57
Indigenous communities 9, 16, 22, 37, 38, 39
Indigenous education 13
Indigenous languages 9, 16, 36, 37, 38, 75
Indigenous peoples 20, 37, 39
Indigenous socio-semiotics 20
infinite category 15–16, 17, 18
Informed by diverse approaches and experiences, element of CREDIBLE approach 31, 35, 36, 39, 40, 66, **91–92**
intelligences 8, 162
Intercultural Communicative Competence (ICC) 86–87, 90–92, **91–92**, **93**, **97**
international representations 153

Kids Guide to Art in Camden 123–130, *126*, *127*, *128*, *129*
Kings Game 139, 146
Know Your Overseas Student Health Cover (OSHC) 67–69, *67*, *68*
knowledge 15–18; commonsense 138; infinite nature of 15–16;

local *see* local knowledge; prior 49, 138; production of 6, 8, 14, 15
Kriol *37*, 37, 39
Kristang community 21, 74, 75
Kristang language 21, 74, 75; endangerment of 43, 76–77, *76*, *77*; prestige of 78–80, *79*

language descriptions 74
language education **92**, 137, 139, 179, 182
language learning 136, 138, 140, 146, 147, 148, 179, 181
language shift 76
language skills 6, 27, 139, 140, 146, 148, 177, 179, 180, 182, 183
Language Travellers 74, 79, 81
Language Travels 21–22, 43, 74–75, *75*, 76–77, *76*, *77*; other iterations of 80–81, *80*; positive outcomes of 77–81, *79*, *80*
language workshops **75**, 78–79
languages: Chinese 9, 111, 148, 160; endangered 74; Indigenous 9, 16, 36, 37, 38, 75; Kristang 21, 43, 74, 75, 76–77, *76*, *77*, 78–80, *79*; local 36, 41, 60, 148; Malay 76, *79*, 79; Ngaanyatjarra *37*, 37, 39; Pitjantjatjara *37*, 37; Putonghua 140, 148; Sasak 9, *10*, 80, 81
lead-in stage, in gender stereotypes in fairy tales workshop 153, 155, 158, 161–162
Leads the field/discipline, element of CREDIBLE approach *31*, 35, 36, 37, 39, 40, **92**
learning 6–7, 10, 24–25, 32, 41; language 136, 138, 140, 146, 147, 148, 179, 181; resources for 45–46, 55, 125–126
Li Hu Ming Xuan 60, 102, *104*, **110**
life, lack of definition of 19–20
light 22, 23
linguistic confidence 90, 92, 137, 138–139, 141–142, 145
linguistic diversity 74, 179
listening 7, 8, 183

literacy: critique of 11–12; definition of 6; education based on 9–10, 14; as goal of education 6–7; reflection 137–138
literature review 71–72, 104, 105, **118**, 126–127, **158**; *see also* analysis of literature; *How to Write: A Literature Review for Project Development*
LNGS 7002: Language, Society, and Power 66, 121
LNGS 7102: Educational Linguistics 45, 46, 50
local context 8, 25
local knowledge 8–9, 11, 31, 35, 36, 39, 40, 66, **91**, **118**, 124, 137, 179
local languages 36, 41, 60, 148
local needs 8, 10, 14, 25, 38, 39

Malaccan Portuguese Eurasian Association (MPEA) 75
Malay 76, *79*, 79
male characters 154, 162
Maleficent 155, **158**, 158, 167; compared to *Sleeping Beauty* 167–168
Mandarin 60, 139–140, 177, 181
masculinist culture 162–163
material design: for Garbage Sorting project 108–109, *109*, **110–111**; for The Ribbit-Ribbit Pond project 95–98, **96**, **97–98**
material development: for Cantonese dialect maintenance project 182–183; for Cards for Courage project 140–141; for Gender Stereotypes in Fairy Tales project 157–159, **158**; for Kids Guide to Art in Camden project 126–129, *127*, *128*
material senses 22, **95**, 108, 109, 114, **117**; and garbage sorting project 105, **110–111**; Group A **23**, 23, 24, 25; Group B **23**, 23, 24; *see also* sight; smell; sound; taste; touch
material-biological world 19, **20**, 20–21, 22, 28
maternal love 168

media 3, 4, 14, 24, 27, 35, 148; multi- 157–158, 181, 182; omni- 180, 181; social 27, 63, 105
methodology 181; for project development 53; *see also* Intercultural Communicative Competence (ICC); Situational Language Teaching (SLT)
micro-economy 21, 75, 78
migrants 21, 55, 87, **91**, **92**, 93, **93**, 94, **97**, **98**
milk tea 69
mindfulness 37, 38–39
mistakes, fear of making 136, 138, 139, 140, 141, 142, 150
modern-colonial education 3–4
motivation 22, 73, 138, 167, 180
MPEA (Malaccan Portuguese Eurasian Association) 75
multimedia 157–158, 181, 182
multimodality 90, 138, 155, 156
myth of the post-colonial 5–6

narrative structure and genre theory 90
narratives 48, 90, 136, 139, 140, 141, **148**, 151, 152, 157, 167
narrow Positive Discourse Analysis (narrow PDA) 32, 51–52
National Education Curriculum 25
National Gallery of Victoria (NGV) 125–126
Ngaanyatjarra 37, 37, 39
NGV (National Gallery of Victoria) 125–126
North Lombok Language Travels 81

objectification, of women 164
observing 7, 99, 113
omnimedia 180, 181
online teaching, supporting of 46–50, 47, **49**, 50
oppression 6, 16, 32, 166
Overseas Student Health Cover (OSHC) 67–69, 67, 68

parental mindsets 138–139
Parra Gonzalez, Ivan Ignacio 86, 90, 93, **93**, 97

participating 7, 148, 160, 166, 182, 183
past tense 27
patriarchy 153–154, 163, 164, 166
PDA *see* Positive Discourse Analysis (PDA)
pedagogy 48, **92**, 138, 156, 157, 179, 181
perceptions 21, 28, 151, 152, 154, 179
performance 6, 75, 80, 141–142, 145–146, 181
phonetics 9–10, 35, 36, 81, 181
picture book 69–70, 69; *see also* The Ribbit-Ribbit Pond
Pinyin, Chinese 60, **187**
Pitjantjatjara 37, 37
poetry 179–180, 181, 182; Cantonese 177, 178, 181, 183, 184; Tang 180
positive change 87, 88, 111
Positive Discourse Analysis (PDA) 31–32, 45, 46, 51–52, 58, 63–64, 88–89, **89**, 90, 99; analysing things form template **115–116**; broad *see* broad Positive Discourse Analysis (broad PDA); designing things form template **116–117**; narrow 32, 51–52; of The Ribbit-Ribbit Pond 93, **93–94**, 95, **96**, 97, **97–98**, 98, **98**
post-colonial, myth of the 5–6
Power of the Poem, The 179–180
PPP ("Presentation", "Practice", "Production") 155
practice 155, 158; pilot 159, 160, 163–166; subaltern 4, 14, 21, 26, 27, 30, 39, 152
pre-implementation 99, **117**
presentation 154, 155, 158, 162–163
"Presentation", "Practice", "Production" (PPP) 155
prestige of Kristang 78–80, 79
prestige planning 75, 78
prince, in Snow White 166
prior knowledge 49, 138
production 155, 158, 167–168; knowledge 8, 14

project goals 53, 55, 57, 109, 114
project review 87, 88, 103, 107, 108
prompts 125, 126, 129, 181
public art 123, 124–125, *128*, 129
Putonghua 140, 148

Racial and gender ideologies in 4 Disney/Pixar featured animations 155–156
rainbow symbol 156
reading 4, 8, 12, 25, 41, 87, **91**, 136, 146, 156, 159
reading/writing 1, 3, 6, 8, 12, 24, 140, 148
real world *31*, 32, 45, 66
recycling 43, 59, 61, 63, 64, 102, 104
reduce your sugar intake 69–70, *69*, *70*
referential skills 180
reflection 26, 87, **93**, **98**, **119**, 130, 136, 142, 160, 177, 184
reflection literacy 137–138
register analysis 52
reliability 26–27, 31
resemanticisation 137–138
respect *10*, 12, 41, 93; mutual 168; self- 41
Responds to practical needs, element of CREDIBLE approach *31*, 34, 36, 38, 40, **91**, 152
reuse, choose to 61–63, *62*
Ribbit-Ribbit Pond, The 21, 83, **85**, 85–101, *86*, **89**, **91–92**, **93–94**, *95*, **95**, **96**, **97–98**, *100*, *101*
romantic love 168

Sasak community 81
Sasak language 9, *10*, 80, 81
science: boli is 11; colonial 15, 16, 17, 18; material-biological 19; social 19, 21
SCOLAR (Standing Committee on Language Education and Research) 139, 147
self-esteem 41, 138
self-respect 41
senses, material *see* material senses
sensory systems 22–24, **23**; and education 24–27; Group A **23**, 23, 24, 25; Group B **23**, 23, 24; sequencing of 23–24

Sequoyah 35–36
SFL (Systemic Functional Linguistics) 51, 52
sight **23**, 23, 24; Ascending Stork Building **187**; Australian anti-tobacco campaign 34; Cards for Courage project **147**, **148**; garbage sorting project **106**, **111**; The Ribbit-Ribbit Pond **94**
single-use coffee cups 59, 61–62, 63, 102
skills 8, 26, 77, 92, 138; language 6, 27, 139, 140, 146, 148, 177, 179, 180, 182, 183; of *Snow White* 164, 166
slave labour 166
Sleeping Beauty 151, **158**, 158, 167; compared with *Maleficent* 167–168
slides 153, 157–158, 159
slow-looking 125
smell **23**, 23, 24; Ascending Stork Building **187**; Australian anti-tobacco campaign 32, 33, **34**; Cards for Courage project **147**, **148**; garbage sorting project **106**, **111**; The Ribbit-Ribbit Pond **94**
Smiling Mind meditation app 36–39, *37*
smoking, in Australia 31, 32, 33, **34**, 34, 35, 88
Snow White 151–152, 154, 155, **158**, 158, 162, 163; historical context of 165–166; interpretation of 163–165; the prince in 166; retelling ending of 167, 168; scenes from 165; social factors shaping 166
social cognitive theory 154
social factors, shaping *Snow White* 166
social marketing 104, 110
social media 27, 63, 105
social sciences 19, 21
societal beliefs 151
socio-semiotic beliefs 21
socio-semiotic dependency 27
socio-semiotic violence 9, 28
socio-semiotic world 18, 19, **20**, 20–21, 22, **23**, 30
socio-semiotics 7, **20**, 21, 22, 24, 27, 32, 33, 35; for betterment 39, *40*,

41; colonial 5, 20; community 85; definition of 4; Indigenous 20
sorting 11, 15–16, 16–17, 18; of garbage 43, 59–61, *60*, *61*
sound 23, *23*, 24; Ascending Stork Building **187**; Australian anti-tobacco campaign 33, **34**; Cards for Courage project **147**, **148**; garbage sorting project **106**, **111**; The Ribbit-Ribbit Pond 93, **94**; and writing systems 9
speaking 8, 136, 137, 139–140, **147**, 147, 148, 150, 177, 183
speech 1, 7, 8, 13, 24, 28, 180
stakeholders *see* Engages stakeholders, element of CREDIBLE approach
standards 26, 46, *47*
Standing Committee on Language Education and Research (SCOLAR) 139, 147
stereotypes, gender 151–160, *156*, *157*, **158**
storytelling 139, 141–142, 147, 150, 152, 163, 180, 182
structural/functional analysis 16–17
subaltern practice 4, 21, 26, 27, 30, 39, 152; definition of 14
successful projects 32, 88–89, 114; *see also* Australian anti-tobacco campaign
sugar intake, reduce your 69–70, *69*, *70*
Sunny Boy 3, 7, 8, *14*, 24–25, 27, 28, 29, 46, 53, 126
supporting online teaching 46–50, *47*, **49**, *50*
Sydney University Postgraduate Representative Association (SUPRA) 67
syllabic writing systems 9, 35, 36, 81
symbols 9, 19, **20**, **23**, 28, 48, 166; visual 6, 9, 156, *157*, 163–164, **187**
Symbols: A Translingual Poem 28, 29
Systemic Functional Linguistics (SFL) 51, 52

Tang poetry 180
target community 48, 53, 60, 61, 62, 63, 69, 72, 86, 88, 90, 97, 103, 104, 107, 114, 115

taste **23**, 23, 24; Ascending Stork Building **187**; Australian anti-tobacco campaign 32, 33, **34**; Cards for Courage project **147**, **148**; garbage sorting project **106**, **111**; The Ribbit-Ribbit Pond **94**
Teaching Learning Cycle (TLC) 51, 52–53, *52*, *53*
teaching resources 65, 139–140, 146, *147*, 147–148, **148**
template: for CREDIBLE report **118–119**; PDA-analysing things form **115–116**; PDA-designing things form **116–117**
textbooks 8, 25, 26, 27, 41, 137, 140, 141, 146
texts 4, 8, *10*, 12, 26, 27, 88, 90, **148**, 156
theoretical framework, for Gender Stereotypes in Fairy Tales project 154–155
theorisation 1, 16, 137
thoughts 15, 18, 20, 28, 37
timelines 86, 99, 103, 113, 115, **158**
TLC (Teaching Learning Cycle) 51, 52–53, *52*, *53*
tobacco 31, 32–35, *33*, **34**
touch **23**, 23, 24; Ascending Stork Building **187**; Australian anti-tobacco campaign 32, 33, **34**; Cards for Courage project **147**, **148**; garbage sorting project **106**, **111**; The Ribbit-Ribbit Pond **94**
tourism 75, 77, 126
translanguaging 90, 92
Trash Project 70–72, *71*
two worlds 19–22, **20**

unachievable goals 18
University of Sydney 43, 45, 61, 66, 67, 83, 86, 102, 121, 155; Union (USU) 62
Urdu 28, 160
USU (University of Sydney Union) 62
Uti Kulintjaku project 38, 39

validity 27, 31
violence 25, 27; socio-semiotic 9, 28
visual symbols 6, 9, 156, *157*, 163–164, **187**

Index

waste sorting poster **106**
websites 68–69, 88; Free Linguistic Conference (FLC) 72, 75, 99, 101
wellbeing, CREDIBLE projects for 66–73, *67*, *68*, *69*, *70*, *71*
workshop design 151–160, *156*, *157*, **158**
world: making sense of the 18–19; material-biological 19, **20**, 20–21, 22, 28; real *31*, 32, 45, 66; socio-semiotic 18, 19, **20**, 20–21, 22, **23**, 30
writing system 8; boli to 9–11, *10*; phonetic 9–10, 35, 36, 81; syllabic 9, 35, 36, 81

YouTube video course 155, 156–157